THE UPSTART GUIDE TO
OWNING AND MANAGING A TRAVEL SERVICE

THE UPSTART GUIDE TO
OWNING AND MANAGING A TRAVEL SERVICE

Dan Ramsey

UPSTART PUBLISHING
Specializing in Small Business Publishing
a division of Dearborn Publishing Group, Inc.

The world is a book.
Those who do not travel, read only a page.
—St. Augustine

Executive Editor: Bobbye Middendorf
Managing Editor: Jack Kiburz
Cover Design: Paul Perlow Design

© 1995 by Dan Ramsey

Published by Upstart Publishing Company, Inc.,
a division of Dearborn Publishing Group, Inc.

Printed in the United States of America

95 96 97   10 9 8 7 6 5 4 3 2 1

Library of Congress Cataloging-in-Publication Data
Ramsay, Dan, 1945–
    The upstart guide to owning and managing a travel service / by Dan
  Ramsey.
     p.   cm.
  Includes index.
  ISBN 0-936894-83–0 (pbk.)
    1. Travel agents—Vocational guidance   I. Title.
G154.R36   1995   95-6816
338.4'791'02373—dc20   CIP

CONTENTS

FOREWORD

by Dorothy Bozulich
Reedsport Travel

With a great deal of pleasure, I remember January 19, 1987. My husband and I stood proudly in front of our newly purchased travel agency while the local newspaper photographer took our picture. This was our first entrance into the world of small business.

We had spent many weeks researching the purchase of an operating travel agency in our community. We tried to learn as many of the 101 things we needed to know before opening our small business. I wish that we had then all the required information in one compact book such as this one. It would have saved us many hours as well as a couple of costly mistakes.

You have the benefit of our experience as well as that of many other successful travel agencies within the pages of this book. Many kudos to Dan Ramsey for providing this valuable assistance.

Enjoy!

PREFACE

The world of travel services is a major industry. It is also a major business opportunity. Between the individual and the multibillion dollar airlines and hotel chains stands the travel service. It is a vital component of the travel industry.

Though many will say that you must have vast financial resources to start a travel service, it isn't so. In fact, many people are finding success in travel services with much less. How? They find and serve a small market, starting on limited funds and growing as the market grows.

That doesn't mean that owning and managing a travel service is a get-rich-quick business. It isn't. Those who try to tell you it is are misrepresenting it. However, many people have proven that you can start a successful travel service with less than $10,000 in cash or credit and can become profitable within a year. This book will show you how.

Maybe you've always dreamed of owning a travel service. Or maybe you're in love with travel and want to share its pleasures with others. Of course, it takes more than love to make a marriage and it takes more than love to make a business. It also takes knowledge and hard work to succeed.

In business, it's not what you know that makes you succeed but what you *don't* know that reduces your chances of success. So success comes from discovering what it is that you don't know about your chosen business opportunity and learning it. Maybe it's a lack of management experience, or financial background, or technical knowledge, or money. Or maybe it's a little bit of each of them.

The Upstart Guide to Owning and Managing a Travel Service is your guide to success with your own small business. As the author of more than 50 business and consumer books, and a small business consultant, I will guide you through the proven steps to starting and operating your own travel service business. I will show you how to set your prices, build your business, pay your taxes, and enjoy what you do. You will also meet successful travel service owners and learn from them.

The Upstart Guide to Owning and Managing a Travel Service includes worksheets, samples and examples to help you start faster and arrive sooner. "Action Guidelines" at the end of each chapter help you quickly apply what you've learned.

A successful travel service can be helpful to others and profitable to you. *The Upstart Guide to Owning and Managing a Travel Service* will help you do both.

ACKNOWLEDGMENTS

Thanks to many people who contributed to the development of this book. They include Dorothy Bozulich of Reedsport Travel; American Society of Travel Agents; Richard Harrison of Buckingham Travel Group; Tom Barrett and Ken Butdorf of Eagle Travel; Spencer Smith, Karen Billipp, and Jean Kerr of Upstart Publishing; David H. Bangs, Jr., author of *The Business Planning Guide*; Lori Capps and Roy L. Fietz of the Business Development Center at Southwest Oregon Community College; and The Small Business Administration Office of Business Development.

Business forms in this book were produced using Per-FORM Forms Designer from Delrina Technology Inc. and Key Draw! Plus from SoftKey Software Products Inc.

OPPORTUNITIES FOR TRAVEL SERVICES

S ome people love to travel. Others must travel for business. Travelers go to vacation spots, conventions, and grandma's house. Travel is important to business and pleasure.

The travel industry includes airlines, cruise ships, trains, bus companies, rental car agencies, travel wholesalers, and tour companies. It also encompasses hotels, motels, bed-and-breakfasts, and other innkeepers. In addition, the travel industry includes tourist centers, passport offices, and government services for the traveler.

Between the traveler and the travel industry are the women and men who provide travel services: trip planning, tour guiding, ticket sales, and travel information and advice. They are knowledgeable, helpful, and hardworking. They are big businesses and small.

The biggest players are American Express/Thomas Cook, Carlson/Wagonlit, Rosenbluth International, and Maritz Travel. In 1994, the largest travel service, American Express,

1

merged with the third-largest agency, Thomas Cook. Their combined sales in the U.S. total nearly $6 billion. Travel is truly big business. It is also small business!

Meet Franklin Travel

Franklin Travel is a two-agent travel service located in northern California. Its clients are primarily small businesses in the area. Owner Maria Franklin had 11 years of experience as a travel agent for a large chain of travel services before opening her own business. Maria's husband, Frank, owns a small business that required frequent travel to clients and conventions. Maria saw a market for special travel services needed by similar businesses in the area and decided to open her own service. That was three years ago. Today, Franklin Travel bills more than $1.2 million in travel services each year. Her business is profitable. Most important, Maria loves her job.

Franklin Travel's office, located in a small business complex, opens its doors at 8:30 A.M., but Maria is there before 8:00 A.M. on most mornings. On her way to work, Maria picks up the mail at the post office and a copy of the metro newspaper. Maria listens to the radio news on her way to the office to catch the headlines, then scans the newspaper for information that will impact the traveler that day: weather, political coups, and the value of the dollar abroad.

One morning, Franklin Travel's answering system had two messages. The first was from a client in Atlanta who called to ask for a change on his return ticket. Maria immediately had the change made and called him back. The second call was from a travel representative for a national convention center with answers to questions Maria called in the day before. Franklin Travel was coordinating reservations for a contingent of conventioneers from northern California to Atlantic City.

Maria quickly scanned the mail for ticket packages, then left the brochures for her travel associate to review and file.

The telephone soon began ringing. Franklin Travel has four telephone lines: two for voice, one for the computer, and one for the fax machine. In addition, an answering system takes messages when both voice lines are busy. Maria believes that a customer who hears a busy signal is a lost opportunity.

Before lunch, Maria handled 18 telephone calls, offering information, planning itineraries, calling clients who have completed trips, and talking with travel representatives. Maria used her lunch hour to make a presentation to a Kiwanis luncheon on how to reduce travel costs. She has made this speech to many local service groups that have high business memberships and has picked up at least one new client at each talk.

On returning from lunch, Maria's associate updated her on a call from a client who is staying in Tokyo. The client was upset with the hotel about a change in room rates. Fortunately, Maria sends most of her Tokyo business travelers to the same hotel and has some clout with management. A telephone call to the hotel manager and one to the client settled the matter and built customer relations.

An afternoon at her desk, on the computer and the telephone, resulted in confirmed itineraries and reservations for two owners of a local business who wanted to simultaneously visit an important new client. Because both owners are critical to the success of the small business, they preferred not to travel on the same flight. A rare accident would destroy the growing business. So Maria had one owner flying out of San Francisco and through Denver while the other flies from Sacramento and through Atlanta to both meet in Boston.

Specializing in business travel isn't all business. Executives want to take a vacation, want to take a spouse or friend along on a business trip, or just want to use up their frequent-flier miles. Franklin Travel also plans trips to the Caribbean, Disney World, Alaska, Las Vegas, and other vacation points. In fact, a growing service for Franklin Travel is offering get-away packages designed for the needs of business owners.

Dealing with businesses is different than dealing with consumers. Business travelers expect preferential treatment. They want immediate, yet personalized service. This pace makes Maria's days hectic, but she prefers it over selling travel to consumers. She also knows that a business travel agency typically sells more travel than a consumer agency.

What a Consumer Travel Service Does

As you can see, not all travel services serve all types of clients. The largest agencies do, but smaller travel agencies typically succeed by selecting a specific market and specializing in serving its needs.

A consumer travel service specializes in advising and serving the consumer travel market. This includes individuals, couples, families, and groups. In fact, some small agencies in large metro areas may specialize in serving group travelers, such as churches or fraternal organizations.

Some agencies focus more on required travel—such as holiday and event travel—while others focus more on adventure travel. One successful metro travel service works primarily with sports fans who want to follow their teams. Another specializes in honeymoon travel for newlyweds. Of course, these travel services will help other consumers, but their primary income is earned through their specialty.

Another popular special travel market is destination travel. That is, an agency in New England may specialize in travel to Florida or the Caribbean during the winter and from many eastern cities to New England in the fall and spring. A destination travel service can be located in the market or at the destination. So a travel service for Chicagoans who want to ski in the Colorado Rockies can be located in Chicago or Vail. It could even be located in Kansas City and advertise a toll-free number in Chicago newspapers.

Depending on your background and interests, consumer travel services may be a good specialty for you. To learn more about consumer travel services, read the travel section of metro newspapers in your state.

What a Business Travel Service Does

Business Week reports that corporate travel is a $100-billion-a-year business. Salespeople must go to clients. Executives need to travel to branch offices. Engineers are required to go to customer sites. Travel services that cater primarily to the business traveler typically sell more travel than consumer agencies. They also work harder.

Business travel services, too, specialize in a part of the market. One agency may work primarily with businesses within a specific industry while another specializes in a popular business destination. Some agencies even set up a branch office at a large client's office to serve their travel needs.

Disadvantages of specializing in business travel include lower commissions, requirements to bill the client, additional services required, time-oriented problems, and intensive competition. Businesses sometimes require a 2–4 percent rebate on all business placed through the agency.

Owning and managing a business travel service will appeal to those who have extensive experience traveling for business. They know the problems that the business traveler faces. They also know what special services will help customers: laptop computer rentals, automatic ticket upgrades, and preferential treatment. Most important, business travelers want to be treated as special individuals who have preferences and peeves. Knowing how to handle business clients can be lucrative.

What a Tour Agent Does

Most consumer and business travelers select a specific destination—Monte Carlo, Mazatlan, Memphis. Others want to travel to many destinations on a single trip. They want to tour.

A tour agent or travel service specializing in tours can build a lucrative business with unique tours for a specific market. The tours may be of Germany for Americans of German descent, or low-impact adventures for senior citizens. The tour can be built around a specific activity, such as skiing, or a destination, like the Greek Islands.

There are two general types of tours: independent and escorted. An independent tour gives the traveler freedom to roam. It gets him or her to the destination, provides housing if desired, and little more. Independent tours appeal to independent travelers and to those on a budget. An escorted tour includes a guide who helps travelers get the most from their experience. Depending on design and destination, an escorted tour may plan every moment of the trip, or it may leave some free time for exploration.

Of course, an escorted tour will cost the traveler more than an independent tour. The costs of the guide and additional services must be covered. Some tour agents not only book the tour but also serve as the tour guide. Becoming a tour agent may appeal to you if you have knowledge or experience with a specific type of client or a regional destination. Tours can be designed for experiencing the Pacific Northwest, coastal Texas, the Andes, or windsurfing off Africa.

One disadvantage to selling tour travel services is that you may have all your eggs in one basket. That is, if you spend three months planning and selling a tour that must be cancelled (weather, funding, strike), your business may quickly fold. Those who want to specialize in tour services typically start by selling tours for others before they attempt to manage a tour of their own.

Travel Is Big Business!

As you can see, travel is big business. In fact, travel agents do nearly $50 billion in business each year. Fortunately, you don't have to own a big travel service to have a successful one. This book will help you to realistically plan and build your business.

If you have not worked in the travel industry, you may be surprised to learn that most travel agents are accredited. They are members of trade associations and industry groups. You'll learn about these groups in Chapter 3. Fortunately, you don't have to be a member of any of them to start your travel service. The coming pages will show you how legitimately to start your own travel service with the help of other travel agencies.

Travel Services in the Information Age

As you can see, a travel service thrives on data and details: flight information, rates and tariffs, customer preferences, geography, and much more. Fortunately, this is the Information Age when data is readily available. In fact, much of the information available to large travel agencies is available to you.

The workhorse of the Information Age is the computer. In the coming pages you'll learn what information is available to you and how to get it. You'll learn how to research and book flights and tours using your computer, even at home.

There's a downside to the availability of so much information on travel: it's overwhelming. You'll also learn how to sort through the data avalanche for the information you need to help your clients. Most important, you'll learn how to offer something your competitors may not be offering: personalized service.

Selecting Your Field of Travel Services

You've seen a variety of travel services that are successfully operated from shopping malls and home offices. Which type of travel service should you offer?

Life is too short to spend it doing something you don't enjoy. Fortunately, there are so many niche or specialty markets that, with thought, you should be able to come up with a list of a dozen or more services from which to choose. Here are some idea starters.

- What popular destination cities or regions are near you?
- Do tourists come to your area? If so, when and why?
- What traveling have you done?
- What destinations or regions have you most enjoyed?
- To what social groups do you belong?
- What has frustrated you about travel?
- If you didn't have to worry about money, what type of travel services would you like to provide for others?
- What are your hobbies and interests?
- Where do people with your hobbies and interests like to travel? When?
- Would you feel more comfortable helping consumer or business travelers?
- Where would you like to work?
- What special knowledge or skills do you have?
- What do you love to do?

The Travel Services Process

Travel services sell other people's products. Travel suppliers include airlines, cruises, trains, buses, tour operators, hotels, car rental agencies, consolidators, wholesalers, and insurance services. (A travel consolidator buys wholesale and sells below retail. A consortium combines member volume for reduced fares or increased commmissions.) You will be selling their services to your clients.

You will produce travel services for others by applying a process. A *process* is a series of operations required in making a product or furnishing a service. The process of making a hamburger, for example, requires knowledge (how to prepare), materials (meat, bun, pickle, special sauce), labor (cooking, assembling, packaging), and results in a specific output (a hamburger) in a form that the customer wants.

There is a process to producing travel services. Understanding the mechanics of the process—the required knowledge, materials, labor, and expected results—will make you a better and more efficient travel agent.

The knowledge required for producing travel services includes: oral and written communication skills, fundamentals of business and economics, geography and travel, a detailed knowledge of the travel industry, and an understanding of your clients' requirements. Your travel service will also be more efficient if you understand business management and the use of computers and software.

The materials you will need for travel services are basic: brochures, tickets, forms, and stationery.

Of course, your travel service will require labor. You will either work as or hire telephone reservation agents or "res agents." In either case, you must understand what the labor requirements of the process are to ensure that the job is being done properly and efficiently.

Finally, you need to define the end result you want. Actually, it is not the final step; it is the first one. Until you understand exactly what your client requires, you cannot define the other elements in your process: knowledge, materials, and labor.

For example, if your travel service primarily provides travel services to the handicapped, your knowledge and contacts are different from the travel service that helps Asians immigrate to the U.S. You cannot efficiently define the components of your process until you have defined your output. In our earlier example, you don't select beef as a material until you've decided that a hamburger is the output or end result you want. You can't make hamburgers using turnips.

All this may sound quite elementary. It is. But it is where more new businesses get lost than anywhere else. They start out with the wrong knowledge, materials, and labor for their clients' needs. They look at their solution before they've even discovered what a client's problem is. They start at the wrong end of the process. This book will guide you in discovering and developing the best—and most profitable—process for your travel service.

Specifically, the process of offering travel services includes the following steps:

- Define client requirements: learn when, where, how, and why the client wants to travel, and any limiting factors.
- Research availability: use your resources to determine what travel services best fit your client's requirements.
- Consult client: discuss the specific options with your client to ensure that they match his or her needs.
- Book travel: with the client's authorization, book the travel arrangements.
- Confirm with client: notify the client of the bookings you have made.

That's the process used by most travel services to help their customers travel efficiently and enjoyably. The details of the process depend on what travel services are offered. For example, a tour agent with a clearly defined market will spend less time on defining requirements and more on booking travel. However, nearly all travel services are developed using this five-step process.

Your Life as a Travel Service Owner

Travel service: It's a business. It's a service. It involves travel. It's fun. It's your life!

Some travel services are an excuse for the owner to travel. Others are so busy that there's no time for travel. Whether the owner takes advantage of them or not, there are many benefits to owning a travel service.

One primary benefit is low-cost travel. Travel agents typically get a 75 percent discount from full airfares. However, this isn't the bargain it seems to be. Most supersaver tickets available to the public are discounted 55 percent from full fare anyway. In addition, most supersaver ticketholders cannot be bumped from a flight while travel agent courtesy ticketholders can. Because of misuse, courtesy tickets also require advance notice and special paperwork.

Fortunately, many travel suppliers, such as tour operators, offer familiarization or "fam" trips at little or no cost. However, they are more like business trips than vacations, requiring that you sit through sales talks and meetings. Even so, owning a travel service can get you out into the world at reduced cost.

What can you expect your life to be like if you decide to become a professional travel agent? That depends. If you're a square peg trying to fit into a round hole, you will be uncomfortable. If you don't enjoy sales, detail work, travel, and working with people in all moods, you will probably be miserable. If you're looking for a way to get rich quickly, try another line of work—one I haven't discovered yet. But if you enjoy helping other people, have good communication skills or a strong desire to develop them, experience in travel or the travel industry, and the need to be an independent business person, furnishing travel services may be a rewarding way of making a living.

How Much Will You Make?

Let's talk about money. The typical travel service has a single office with total annual sales of about $2.5 million. However, the majority of travel agencies are smaller, doing about $1–1.5 million in sales each year. About two-thirds of these travel dollars go toward domestic and international airfares, 15 percent toward cruises, 10 percent toward hotels, and the balance toward car rentals, railroad tickets, tours, excursions, and related services.

Travel services earn their money from commissions paid by travel providers. Commissions are 8–15 percent depending on services provided. Air carriers pay 8–11 percent commission, car rental agencies pay 5 percent, cruise ships pay 12–15 percent, and wholesalers pay an average of 12 percent commission. Some travel services use 10 percent as a guideline, but much depends on what specific services are sold. An agency that specializes in package deals from wholesalers can earn a higher commission than one that primarily sells airline tickets. In addition, higher commissions (called overrides) and bonuses are sometimes offered by travel providers to promote travel during slow seasons or to build new services.

One typical agency booked $1.7 million in a recent year, 40 percent from airline tickets and 48 percent from cruises. They sold fewer airline tickets and more cruises than the average travel service office because airline tickets paid an average of 8 percent commission while cruises paid 14 percent. Good economics!

About 75 percent of all travel agencies report that they are profitable, showing an average profit of about $60,000. How much can you expect to make operating a travel service? Of course, much depends on local need, competition, your skills, and other factors. But there are some guidelines that will get you started.

First, the typical travel service operated by the owner without employees can sell about $350,000 to $600,000 in services in a year. Using an average commission of 10 percent, this travel service would have a net income of $35,000 to $60,000.

How much profit should you expect to make? As a service business, much of your income will go to pay for labor (Figure 1.1, on page 13). In a one-person office, that's you. According to the Small Business Administration, the typical

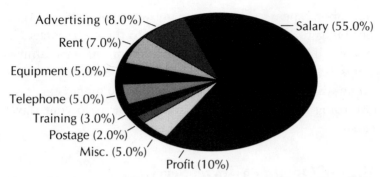

Figure 1.1: Average expenses and profits for a typical travel service's second year of operation

travel service will spend 8 percent on advertising and promotion, 7 percent on rent, 5 percent on equipment and supplies, 5 percent on telephone, 3 percent on training, 2 percent on postage, and another 5 percent on taxes and miscellaneous.

The average established travel agency has 4.4 employees and 2.6 outside agents. Should you add an employee? Only if you are certain that you will increase income by at least *two to three times* the employee's salary. For example, to hire an employee at $20,000 a year (about $10 an hour), make sure the employee's services will bring you at least $40,000–60,000 in commissions ($400,000–$600,000 in sales) during the coming year. That's a minimum. Some service businesses use higher multipliers to determine whether they can afford to hire additional staff. I'll cover finding and hiring good employees later in this book. I'll also describe how you can hire and maintain outside agents on commission rather than salary.

These estimates are guidelines to help you in calculating income, expenses, and profitability. As your business develops you may decide to make your salary a higher percentage of sales and reduce the profit or earnings you retain in the business. Or you may find that you can reduce expenses without reducing income by working from your home. Or you may decide to hire a spouse or friend even though it will increase your labor expense. There are many ways you can fine tune your budget. But, to start, stay as close to these percentages as possible. If you spend too little on promotion, for example, your sales may be dramatically reduced because customers simply won't know about your business. The money spent on advertising is well worth it for drawing clients to your travel service.

Risks of Owning a Travel Service

Certainly, there are many risks involved in starting and running your own business, no matter what type of business it is. But you can minimize these risks by understanding what you're getting into—the purpose of this book—and knowing how to get out of it if you must. Never enter a room without an exit. Chapter 8 will help you discover those exits as well as help you keep from needing to use them.

A major risk to starting your travel service is that you will lose your investment of time and money. How can you minimize these risks? Some travel agents start their service at home in their spare time while working another job. This structure presents a number of challenges, but they can be overcome. The business can depend on an answering service or a relative to handle phone inquiries. In fact, a travel service can turn this limitation to an advantage, offering evening and weekend appointments that competitors do not.

The most successful travel services are those that operate from a retail shop near their clients. This can also be the most expensive operation as rent in a business district can be high. The new travel service can be tempted to locate in a lower-rent area to reduce financial risks. Don't! You'll actually be increasing your financial risks because a poor location will yield a higher percentage of income going to rent. For example, a high-rent office may cost $1,000 a month but bring you $12,000 in commissions in a month, costing about 8 percent of net income while a $400-a-month office may only bring you $2,000 in commissions each month, or 20 percent of net income. The cheaper route can actually increase risk.

An alternative to high rent is shared rent. That is, you may be able to sublease a desk or office from another business. This can be especially effective if the landlord or the person you're sharing space with has a related business with which you can share clients. You'll be increasing income while you reduce risk. I'll cover offices in greater detail in the next chapter.

The best way to minimize risks is to understand what they are and to prepare for those from which you cannot recover. You'll want fire insurance. You'll want sufficient operating capital to get you through the first 6 to 12 months of your business. You'll want only minimal office supplies. You'll want to come up with alternative services to ensure that you have income. You'll want to make sure that any leases you sign can be renegotiated if your business doesn't work out. As suggested earlier, make sure you have sufficient exits before you enter.

Action Guidelines

This introduction to starting your own travel service has given you an overview of the business to help you determine if it is right for you. To help you make that decision, here are some actions you can take today:

✔ Start your travel business notebook, writing down ideas and the answers to Action Guideline questions.

✔ Check your local phone book's Yellow Pages under "Travel Agencies and Bureaus" and "Tours" to see who your competition might be. Visit them.

✔ Read the travel section of newspapers in your area to determine who is offering travel services and how they advertise.

✔ Select one or two leading travel services in your area and call them to learn more about their services.

✔ Do some rough calculations of your potential income and expenses based on guidelines in this chapter.

✔ Make a list of the risks you would face by starting your own travel service.

✔ Talk to others about your ideas to get fresh perspectives on them.

TRAVEL SERVICE
REQUIREMENTS

W hat do you need in order to own and manage a successful travel service? Many things. Understanding what the requirements are and how to meet them will help you ensure the success of your new business.

This chapter outlines and describes those requirements. They include reviewing your personal and financial goals and values, specific tools and equipment, and numerous travel industry resources. In addition, you'll. find free resources offered by the government to help your business succeed.

Some of the knowledge and skills required to own and manage a successful travel service are:

- Knowledge of geography, cultures, history, and world events
- Knowledge of how to get along with people
- Time management skills
- Ability to remember details

- Ability to find the answer to nearly any question
- Imagination and creativity

If you don't have all these skills, work to develop them. You may decide that you don't have sufficient experience to open your own travel service yet but will do so soon. Find a job in a travel service or in the travel industry; build your skills and experience toward the day when you can open your own travel service.

There's another vital component of your success: a personal desire to help others. This is important if you are an employee; it is vital if you are the owner. As consumers, we can easily read the attitude of people who serve us. We know when someone is helping us because it's their job or because they enjoy doing their job. And we usually respond by supporting and recommending those who help us solve our problems and make us feel important. They appreciate our business—and they get it.

Before you decide whether operating a travel service is for you, you must know who *you* is. What do you feel most comfortable doing? Under what conditions do you enjoy working with people? Under what conditions do you prefer to avoid people? What are your personal goals? What are your financial goals? How much risk do you feel comfortable taking? Most important, is a travel service a good fit in your life or will it cause more problems than it cures? Self-analysis can be difficult, but it is the only way of ensuring that this or any other goal will bring you the results you want in your life.

Your Personal Goals

Maybe by this stage in your life you've developed a list of personal goals for the next year, five years, and beyond. Most people have not. It isn't mandatory that you develop a long list of your life's goals before you start a travel service or other business, but it will increase your chances of personal and financial success.

A *goal* is an objective. It is somewhere you want to be or something you want to have. It can be the goal of owning your own travel service. Or it may be the option of working at home. Or it can be amassing $1 million in assets within 20 years to fund your retirement. Whatever they are, they are your personal goals and they reflect who you are and what you want from your life.

These are questions to help you determine your personal goals and how you can fulfill them.

- What are your personal goals?
- Why do you think you want to own a travel service?
- Do you like the independence of owning a business?
- Are you searching for a career change and feel that the travel industry is a good option?
- Are you starting a business because you want to make your own job rather than work for someone else?
- Are you primarily interested in starting a travel service to make money?
- Are you looking for a way of finding and funding low-cost travel?
- Are you searching for something to do during retirement?

Your Personal Values

Values are tools that will take you toward your personal goals. Values are standards or qualities that you've established to help you make daily decisions. Those people who succeed in any business have some common personal values. Let's look at those values together to determine your strengths and opportunities.

Self-awareness. The process of starting and operating any business is difficult. It will require that you constantly test yourself, maintaining what works and changing what doesn't. But that's what many people love about being a business owner: the endless challenges. It makes them aware of their characteristics and requires that they continue to grow.

Hard work. The great thing about being an independent businessperson is that you get to select which *12 hours* of the day you're going to work! It's true. As you start and grow your travel business, you'll spend at least eight hours a day producing your product and another two to six hours marketing and administrating it. Don't expect to work just a 40-hour week— at least for awhile—and you won't be disappointed.

Discipline. Discipline is the power behind hard work. You can know exactly what needs to be done and still not do it. Self-discipline forces you to act. Having goals that are meaningful to you will increase your self-discipline.

Independence. Great business owners often make poor employees. They're too independent. That's alright. They cannot, however, be stubborn. Business owners must maintain a balance between independence and open-mindedness to succeed.

Self-confidence. It takes a lot of nerve to start a business. It takes a lot more to make it successful. But nerve or self-confidence isn't ego. It's a belief in your unique skills founded on past success. You know you can successfully operate a travel service because you have the skills to do so, not just the desire.

Adaptability. Life is chaos. No matter how much we plan, people and events change. Products change. Markets change. We change. A successful business owner must adapt to these changes. Without change, life becomes very dull.

Judgment. To succeed in business, you must make good decisions every day. Wisdom requires knowledge. You must be able to gather complete and accurate facts and make the best decision you can from those facts. You will not be right every time, but you will be right most of the time. This is good judgment.

Stress tolerance. Stress is defined as "the confusion created when one's mind overrides the body's basic desire to clobber some yo-yo who desperately deserves it. " Humor can help reduce stress. Stress is a part of everyday life, especially in business. Learning to live with stress without taking it personally can help you succeed in business.

Need to achieve. Success is the achievement of something you go after. It may be the completion of a project, or the start of a business, or the learning of a new skill. This need is a driving force within successful business owners that helps give them the energy to reach their goal.

Your Financial Goals

As much as you may love producing travel services and helping people, you must also have financial goals. Without a fair salary and profit, you won't be able to help people for very long.

What is an appropriate financial goal for your travel service? One that funds your other goals. If your business goal is to open a new travel service office each year for three years, your financial goal must be one that will fund such an ambitious goal. If your business goal is to build a successful travel service then sell it in ten years and retire, your financial goal must match the expected selling price of your business. If your business goal is to make a good salary as well as a fair return on your investment, you must first determine what a good salary and a fair return mean to you.

One successful travel service owner established a financial goal of developing annual sales of $500,000 within one year, then bring his daughter into the business. His longer-term goal is to sell the business to his daughter and retire within ten years. He then wanted to travel full-time. His goals are specific and attainable.

Your Risk Tolerance

Business is legalized gambling. When you start a business, you're gambling that you will succeed. You're also facing the risk that you will fail and face personal and financial loss. How much does this risk bother you? How much risk can you tolerate?

Everyone's risk tolerance level is different. Some people cannot afford to lose a dime. Of course, as they say in Las Vegas: "One who can't afford to lose can't afford to gamble." Others say: "I started with nothing. Anything I get is a gain." Still others determine potential losses and say: "It's worth the gamble, but I'm going to do whatever I can to improve the odds."

You must determine your own risk tolerance and that of those with whom you share your life. If you're ready to take the plunge, but your spouse would rather not, find a mutually acceptable level of risk before starting your business. Otherwise, you may find—as too many people have— that you've traded an invaluable relationship for a replaceable business.

Tools and Equipment You Will Need

There are a variety of tools available that can make your travel service more efficient and more profitable. They include office furniture, computers, software, printers, copiers, reference books, answering machines, fax machines, and stationery. Here's how successful travel services select these vital tools.

Office Furniture

Depending on where you locate your travel service and how you plan to interact with your customers, you will need office furniture. As a guideline, you will need one desk, office chair, and four-drawer filing cabinet for each agent in your office. If customers will visit your office, you will also need an average of two comfortable chairs for each agent's desk.

You may also want a reception area with a receptionist's desk and chair plus chairs or a sofa. The quality of your office furniture depends on whether you're trying to impress customers or not. A travel service that only meets customers on the telephone won't need much beyond functional furniture, especially if it is located in an office in your home. A travel service selling expensive vacations should have furniture to match.

In addition to standard office furniture, you will probably want to decorate your office in cheerful colors. Retail travel services will want space for travel posters and souvenirs. A business travel office will be more businesslike. A list of prominent clients could be displayed in the waiting area.

Depending on your licensing and bonding requirements, you may need to have a safe on-premises for storage of tickets and other valuables.

Computer Hardware

A computer is one of the most valuable tools a travel service can own. A computer can help you efficiently verify schedules, make reservations, check weather conditions, develop sales letters and marketing brochures, and keep track of your income and expenses. It allows you to access a wide variety of travel information using special software and telephone lines. You simply cannot operate a competitive travel service without a computer anymore.

You may decide to lease a computer reservation system (CRS) computer from one of the reservation services (see Chapter 2). If so, they will furnish the computer, software, telephone lines, and other equipment required to access the service. However, some travel services purchase their own computer and software for reservations as well as for other office duties.

People are often apprehensive about computers because of all the new terminology that they must decipher: CPUs, bits, bytes, bauds, networks, boards, hard disks, RAM, monitor interlacing, and on and on. Don't worry about it. You'll quickly pick up what the terms mean. Here's a simplified introduction to computers—or it may be a review. As most business computers are IBM-compatible, that's what I'll discuss. Apple's Macintosh computers use a different operating system, but the basics are the same.

CPUs. A CPU is a central processing unit. It is an electronic machine built around a microprocessor called a *chip*, which processes information for you.

The CPU is typically called by the same name as the microprocessor chip that is its brain. As an example, early PCs (personal computers) used a microprocessor chip called the 8088 (eighty eighty-eight). So they were called 88s or by the IBM brand name for the model, the XT. The next generation microprocessor and CPU was the 80286, referred to as the 286 (two eighty-six) or by the IBM brand model, the AT. Then came the 386, the 486, and the 586—or Intel Pentium microprocessor and CPU.

The next number to remember in looking at CPUs is the *clock speed.* XT chips had a clock speed of about 5 MHz (mega or million hertz). By comparison, today's 486 and newer microprocessors have clock speeds of 50 MHz and more!

You'll also hear the terms SX and DX. Simplified, a 486DX has more processing power than a 486SX. A DX2 is faster than a DX, and a DX4 is even more so.

So all you really need to know about buying a PC is that a 486 is faster than a 286 or 386, a DX2 is faster than an SX or DX, and a clock speed of 66 MHz is faster than one that's 33 MHz. Fortunately, there's not more than a few hundred dollars difference between fast and super-fast.

Hard Disks. The hard disk drives in your PC can hold thousands of pages of information on its stacked disks (that look like miniature LP records stacked on a record player—if you remember what record players look like). The hard disk controller knows where to look for any information you've put into it, and it can give you the information in a small fraction of a second.

The storage capacity of a hard disk is measured by the number of bytes or computer (not English) words that it can store. Actually, capacity is normally measured in millions of bytes, or megabytes (Mb). Older PCs were equipped with hard disks of 10Mb, 20Mb, or 40Mb. Newer PCs can store 120Mb, 240Mb, 500Mb or even one billion bytes, a gigabyte (Gb), or more. That's *one billion* bytes. To put that in terms that are more understandable, a 1Gb hard disk can theoretically store about a half-million typed pages.

RAM. A hard disk is a storage area, much like a library, where millions of pieces of information can be kept. But a computer also needs a work area where information can be opened and used. This place is called the *random access memory* or RAM.

Depending on the size of the programs you will be using, your PC's RAM should be at least 4Mb. Older PCs offered between 1/2 and 1Mb of RAM, but today's PCs typically come with 4 to 32Mb. The larger this work area is, the more work that can be done simultaneously. Some software like Microsoft Windows and Novell NetWare require at least 4Mb and really work better if you have 8Mb of RAM or more.

Diskette Drives. Data can be moved from one PC to another using small, portable diskettes. These diskettes, sometimes called *floppies*, can store from a third of a megabyte to up to nearly three megabytes of information. Once you've developed a file on your hard disk, you can transport the data by instructing the PC to copy it to a diskette.

In the past ten years since PCs have become popular, a number of diskette formats of higher density have evolved. A higher density of magnetic particles allows storage of more information, once the computer's operating system has formatted the diskette. Earlier diskettes were $5^1/4$ inches square, and were made of a thin, round plastic disk placed in a bendable (hence the name floppy) envelope and sealed. As technology has developed, a greater amount of information can now fit on one diskette. Early *single-density* diskettes held 360K (kilo or one thousand bytes), then *double-density* disks stored 720K. *High-density* quickly multiplied storage to 1,200K or 1.2Mb. Many PCs still use the $5^1/4$-inch format.

Another format soon emerged, the $3^1/2$-inch diskette with a thin, round plastic diskette housed in a hard plastic case. Double-density $3^1/2$-inch diskettes hold 720K, and high-density diskettes store 1.44Mb and fit into a shirt pocket!

The storage capacity of a diskette is a function of the computer as well as the diskette. If you buy a used or older computer, make sure it can read high-density diskettes.

Another option is the removable drive. A couple of choices in this area are SyQuest or Bernoulli. They attach to your computer and allow you to place up to 44 or 88Mb of information onto a disk. The disk may be used to back up your data files. This is also an excellent method of storing older files that may be used again, rather than keeping them on your hard drive.

Monitor. You will also require a monitor, similar to a TV screen where the information you're working on is displayed.

A monochrome (black and white) monitor is least expensive. Color monitors are easier to read—and more attractive—but also more expensive. SVGA (super video gate array) monitors are today's cost-effective standard. Rather than get into a boring description of interlacing and pixels, look for a quality monitor that's easy to read. If you can't see the difference between a $300 monitor and one that costs $1,000, don't buy the expensive one. Most monitors require that you buy a separate video card to be installed in the computer. Video cards also have random access memory, called VRAM, to help them display screens quickly.

Computer Software

Now that you understand the basics of computers, you can better see how computer programs work for you. And, even though computer hardware is discussed here first, you will probably select the computer programs or software before you choose the computer or hardware to run it on.

A computer program is a set of instructions written in a language that your computer understands. The program can be as simple as a word processor or as complex as a database. Let's look at the function of each category of computer software.

Operating systems. DOS stands for disk operating system, which comes with your computer and translates commands like COPY into a language that your PC understands. The most widely used DOS is MS-DOS developed by Microsoft Corp. Novell DOS was developed by Digital Research, now owned by Novell. IBM OS/2 is another popular operating system.

Shell programs make your PC easier to use and perform a number of important maintenance functions. It's called a shell because it wraps around the less-friendly DOS program to make it easier to copy, delete, and manage files. Some shell programs also include *utilities* or special programs that help you keep your data organized and safe.

Windows is a program developed by Microsoft that lets you open a number of overlapping boxes or windows on your computer screen, each with different programs in them. You can be writing a letter when a client calls and you quickly switch to a window with information about the client and your current project.

Word Processors. Word processors simply process words. That is, they let you type words into the computer, move them around, insert words, take some out, and make any changes you want before you print them to paper. You can use word processors to write letters to clients and prospects. I've used computer word processors for more than ten years and would never go back to typewriters. Word processors let you change your mind.

Common word processing programs include WordPerfect, Microsoft Word, Ami Pro, WordStar, and XyWrite. Each has its own following and unique features. Some are more user-friendly than others. WordPerfect is one of the most widely used word processors. Ami Pro is probably the friendliest. Microsoft Word is popular for users of Microsoft Windows.

Spreadsheets. A spreadsheet arranges numbers into usable form. It's named after the wide multicolumnar sheets that accountants use to make journal entries. There are many ways you will soon find yourself using a spreadsheet software program.

As an example, you can purchase a basic spreadsheet program for about $100 that will let you enter horizontal rows or lines of job expense categories and vertical columns of numbers. Most important, you can then tell the program to make calculations on any or all of the columns or rows and it will do so in less than a second. If you update a number, it automatically recalculates the total for you.

Fancier and more costly spreadsheets can follow instructions you write, called *macros*, to do special calculations automatically. You may want to write a macro that will select all of the invoices over 60 days due and total them up. Better spreadsheets will also produce fancy graphs and pie charts that impress lenders and other financial types.

Popular spreadsheet programs include Lotus 1-2-3, Borland Quattro Pro, and Microsoft Excel.

Databases. A database software program is much like an index card file box. You can write thousands or even millions of pieces of information and store them. But a database program is even better than a file box because it finds information in the files in a fraction of a second.

The most common application of a database program for travel services is a client file. As you add clients, prospects, and other business contacts, you may soon need at least a simple database program to keep track of them.

Your prospect/client database will keep information about their name, street address, city, state, zip code, phone and fax numbers, contact names, travel preferences, list of travel packages you've built for them, and even their hobbies. Then, if you want to find out how many of your clients are located in a specific city and haven't purchased any services from you in the last year, you simply tell your database program to search its files for you. It's that easy.

Popular database programs include Borland Paradox, Microsoft Access, Lotus Approach, and Microsoft FoxPro. Depending on which word processor and spreadsheet you select, you may want to purchase a database program by the same company. For example, if you use Lotus's Ami Pro and 1-2-3, consider their database program, Approach. The operating logic of each software developer is slightly different from that of other developers, but you'll usually see continuity within product lines.

Integrated Programs. You can also find integrated software programs that combine the three primary programs: word processor, spreadsheet, and database. Ask your local computer store to recommend a good integrated program. Some include other related programs, such as communications software that lets your PC talk to other PCs over the phone using modems. The cost of a good-quality integrated system is usually much less than the total price for the individual components.

Here's another plus to integrated programs: They talk to each other. That is, your word processor can include financial figures from your spreadsheet in your correspondence, and send it by modem to someone listed in your database. Just as important, an integrated group of programs developed by a single software firm will have similar commands in each program. You won't have to learn three separate programs, you'll learn one larger program.

Integrated programs are especially recommended for those who don't want to spend a lot of time selecting and learning numerous software programs. Popular integrated programs include Microsoft Works, ClarisWorks, Lotus SmartSuite, Borland Office, and Microsoft Office.

Vertical Software. In addition to general business software, there are programs and online services developed specifically to help research and book travel services. These systems allow your computer to show you the latest flight and travel information as gathered from larger computers and delivered over a telephone line. These systems include:

> SABRE (American Airlines)
> APOLLO (United Airlines)
> WORLDSPAN (Delta Airlines)

These and other airline computer reservation systems (CRS) can be accessed for a monthly fee plus an equipment lease.

In addition, CompuServe (800-848-8199) offers access to EAASY SABRE, Official Airline Guide Electronic Edition,

WORLDSPAN Travelshopper, Travel Forum, and other resources. Some travel services begin their business using CompuServe, then expand to specific online services for the travel industry as they grow.

Printers

Letters and other business documents must be sent from your computer to a printer to be printed on paper. There are many types of printers to select from. But we only need to cover the basics of them here so you'll know which ones to look for as you go shopping.

Dot Matrix. The dot matrix printer forms letters from a bunch of dots. A 9-pin printer uses nine tiny pins—three rows of three—to form each letter. The 24-pin printer does the same job but uses 24 pins—four rows of six. So the letters formed by a 24-pin printer are easier to read than that of a 9-pin printer. Today, most dot matrix printers use 24 pins.

Laser. A laser is simply a beam of light that's focused by a mirror. A small laser in your printer actually writes the characters by magnetizing a piece of paper, black dust called toner is passed over it and sticks to the places the laser light touched, then the sheet travels through a heater that fuses the black toner to the paper. An LED or light-emitting-diode printer works in virtually the same way.

Bubble Jet. Similar to the laser, the bubble jet printer sprays special ink onto the page in patterns cut by heat. Bubble jet printers are typically less expensive than laser printers.

Which type of printer should you buy? You may be required to purchase a specific type and model in order to print out tickets for your clients. If you use your computer to write letters to clients and to design your own brochures, purchase a laser printer.

Copiers

Copy machines can be very useful to your travel business. You will want to conveniently copy correspondence, forms, itineraries, brochures, confirmations, and other documents. A good copier can be purchased for under $800. If you're producing a client newsletter, your own brochures, direct mail pieces, or other marketing documents, your copy machine can be more cost-effective than running down to the copy shop or printer for a few copies every day.

Features you will want to look for in a copier may include enlargement and reduction, paper trays, collating of multiple copies, and reproduction of photos. Depending on what travel service packages you sell, you may want a copier that can produce duplex or two-sided copies. Or you may want a copier that prints on 11 x 17-inch sheets for professional four-page travel services. Determine your copying needs before you buy.

Fax Machines

There are more than 25 million fax machines in the world. The concept of the fax machine is simple: It reads a sheet of paper for dark spots much like a copy machine does. It then converts these spots into a code that's sent across a telephone line at a speed of nearly 10,000 bits of information per second. Based on international standards, the fax machine on the other end knows how to read these signals and convert them into light and dark spots that conform to the image that was sent. This image is printed on a piece of paper, and you have a facsimile or fax.

The travel agent can now send letters, itineraries, confirmations, literature, copies of invoices, and other printed material to prospects, clients, travel suppliers, wholesalers, and others in just seconds. A typical one-page fax takes less than a minute to transmit on a Group 3 fax machine. Group 3 is the current standard for facsimile machines, established by an international committee for data communication, CCITT. The fax machine, like the computer, is dramatically changing the way that businesses conduct business.

Facsimile machines look like small printers, with a tray to hold outgoing paper and a telephone set either attached or nearby. You call the fax number where you want to send something, and your fax machine sends out a tone that tells the other machine it would like to transmit a facsimile. The receiving machine sends your machine a high-pitched tone, you manually press your machine's start button and hang up the phone. The fax is being transmitted. Some machines automate the process; you simply put the copy into the machine, press a button that calls a specific telephone in memory, and the fax is sent without any outside help.

There are dozens of features to consider when buying a fax machine for your business. However, many are frills. Most important is that your fax machine is Group-3 compatible. Beyond that, explain to the salesperson what you need your fax machine for and let him or her show you the newest features and whistles. You can get a basic fax machine for $300-$400, a better one for $400-$800, and your heart's desire for a thousand dollars or more. Or you can rent or lease a fax machine. This is an especially good idea with products like faxes that quickly become obsolete.

The more expensive fax machines will print on plain paper rather than slick thermal paper that has a tendency to curl and fade. Depending on how you use documents faxed to you and how long you keep them, a plain paper fax may or may not be most economical.

Some fax machines you look at will combine other functions. It may have a standard telephone handset that you can use for your primary or secondary business line. Some also include a tape or digital answering machine. This setup is practical because you have the business phone line feeding into one machine that can serve three purposes: lets you answer, takes messages, and takes and sends faxes. But, like any machine that combines functions, if one goes out or becomes obsolete, they may all go. Compare the cost of a combined unit against the cost of individual units. If there is little difference in total cost, go for the separate components.

If you decide to purchase a computer for your travel business, consider PC fax boards. They are printed circuit boards that are installed inside your computer and allow you to plug in a phone and use it as a fax. There are even models that will serve as your answering machine as well. Fax boards are typically purchased through computer stores. Computer software can let you fax letters, proposals, and other documents directly from your computer without printing them first to paper.

Telephone Service

Businesses have a number of telephone service options available to them. The most popular is the 800 number, available through most long-distance telephone companies. Having an 800 number allows your prospects and clients to call you toll-free. You pay for the call. The advantage is that more people will be inclined to call you. That's also the disadvantage as salespeople will use it to pitch you—on your dime! Toll-free 800 service is available through most long distance carriers for a small monthly charge plus a per-minute charge that is typically higher than standard long distance rates. Call your carrier for more information and fees on 800 service.

Two new telephone services include 700 service and 500 service. Marketed under various trade names, the 700 service lets calls follow subscribers anywhere within 127 countries and areas. If you work from a variety of offices, a 700-prefix telephone number can be useful as the people who need to reach you will be able to. There is typically an enrollment fee and a monthly fee for the service. For more information on 700 service, call AT&T EasyReach at 800-982-8480 or your preferred long-distance carrier.

A 500-prefix telephone number, a new service, automatically routes incoming calls to various locations you select: office, cellular, home, etc. If not picked up at any of the locations, a voice mailbox takes a message from the caller. For more information on 500 service, call AT&T True Connections at 800-870-9222 or your preferred long distance carrier.

Reference Books

There are many valuable reference books to help you manage your travel business. They include:

- *ASTA's Travel Agent Manual* (American Society of Travel Agents, 1101 King St., Alexandria, VA 22314)
- *Business Travel Planner* (Official Airline Guides, 2000 Clearwater Dr., Oakbrook, IL 60521)
- *Official Airline Guide* (Official Airline Guides, 2000 Clearwater Dr., Oakbrook, IL 60521)
- *Official Hotel Guide* (44 Cook St., Denver, CO 80206)
- *Official Tour Directory* (Thomas Publishing, One Penn Plaza, New York, NY 10019)
- The Intrepid Traveler's Complete Desk Reference (Intrepid Traveler, P.O. Box 438, New York, NY 10034)

Some of these resources are also available online through online travel information services listed above.

Financial Requirements

How much money will you need to build a profitable travel service? Figure 2.1, on page 36, will help you make a preliminary estimate of your business's financial requirements. These estimates will be revised and expanded in future chapters.

Financial Worksheet

Estimated Start-Up Costs:

Office preparation	$_____
Office equipment	$_____
Initial office supplies	$_____
Telephone, answering machine	$_____
Utility deposits	$_____
ARC and other memberships	$_____
Licenses & permits	$_____
Insurance and bonds	$_____
Professionals	$_____
Signs	$_____
Initial advertising	$_____
Miscellaneous expenses	$_____
Total Estimated Start-Up Costs	$_____

Estimated Operating Costs:

Living expenses	$_____
Employee salaries	$_____
Rent	$_____
Utilities	$_____
Advertising	$_____
Insurance	$_____
Office supplies	$_____
Taxes	$_____
Equipment maintenance	$_____
Total Estimated Operating Costs	$_____

Estimated Financial Resources:

Assets

Checking and savings	$_____
CDs and securities	$_____
Owed to you	$_____
Real estate	$_____
Autos and vehicles	$_____
Insurance cash value	$_____
Other assets	$_____
Total assets	$_____

Liabilities

Credit cards	$_____
Household credit	$_____
Auto loans	$_____
Taxes	$_____
Education loans	$_____
Mortgages	$_____
Other liabilities	$_____
Total liabilities	$_____
Total net worth	$_____

Figure 2.1: You can easily calculate common travel service start-up and operating costs, and your financial resources using this worksheet.

To estimate start-up costs, you will need to make your best guess of how much it will cost to set up your office for the day you open the front door to your first customer. This includes the cost of preparing and equipping your office, getting required licenses and professional memberships, getting the phone hooked up, and funding your initial advertising.

Estimating operating costs can be difficult because it requires that you estimate your living expenses as well. Most people who have been employees spend as much as they make; they're not sure exactly what they *need* to live on. However, by starting with your current net (after taxes) salary, you can roughly calculate whether you require more or less to live on. If you operate your business as a sole proprietor (discussed further in Chapter 4), your income taxes and self-employment (social security) tax will be paid by the business.

Other operating costs are those expenses that you will pay each month to keep the doors open (fixed or overhead expenses), as well as those that increase as sales increase (variable expenses).

Where can you get the money you need to start your business? A survey of small businesses conducted by Coopers & Lybrand found that 73 percent were funded by the owners and their families, 13 percent by outside investors, 8 percent by banks, and 6 percent by alliances with other businesses. However, the survey reported that the businesses that were owner-financed had the highest failure rate. You'll learn how to use your financial resources—and develop new ones—in Chapter 7.

Fees and Bonds

To own a traditional travel service, you will probably need membership in one or more travel trade associations. They will be covered in greater detail in Chapter 3, which deals with resources for your travel service.

For example, to sell airline tickets you will need membership in the Air Traffic Conference. There is an application fee, an annual agency fee, and performance bond. The International Air Traffic Association also requires an application and entrance fee, as well as an annual agency fee. Other assocations require fees and dues. Why? Because they will help transfer funds between you and the carrier with the least hassle.

Must you be a member of these groups, pay fees, and provide bonds? No. If you work as an independent contractor, called an outside agent, for a member travel agency, you can utilize the agency's membership. We'll discuss this option later in the book.

How to Manage Your Time

How can the travel service business owner ensure that his or her time is well managed? First, by organizing work space so that important papers don't get lost and unimportant papers do. You can also make a rule that you will avoid handling papers more than once. If you pick up a piece of paper, make a decision regarding it right then if possible.

Set up a regular work schedule. It may be from 7 A.M. to 6 P.M. or 8 A.M. to 5 P.M., or 6 A.M. to 6 P.M. Whatever it is, try to stick to it. If you manage your time well, you will be able to. If you have one time of the day that seems more productive for you than others, plan your most important functions around it.

What about travel and waiting time? Take work with you in a briefcase or purchase a laptop computer that you can use to keep productive every minute. As your time management skills improve, you'll learn how to do more than one thing at a time. You could be making job notes or talking with a key employee or gathering information on an upcoming project while you're waiting to talk with a client.

Meetings seem to be one of the biggest time-wasters. But you can change this by thoroughly preparing for all of your meetings. Meetings, to be productive, must have a purpose or

Time and stress are closely related. The lack of time to do what you need to do often increases personal stress. How do you manage both? Following are ideas from a successful travel agent.

- Plan your time and establish priorities on a daily "to do" list.

- Decide what your prime time is and do your most important or difficult tasks then.

- Set business hours, specific times when you're at work and times when you turn on the answering machine because you're on duty but off call. You, your customers, and your family will appreciate knowing your set routine, even though you know that for special events or emergencies you can break that schedule.

- Confirm your appointments one-half day before the appointment—afternoon for next morning or morning for that afternoon. It will save you time, and your clients will appreciate the consideration.

- If you're working from your home, give your business as much of a separate and distinct identity as possible. Although you might save a few dollars by using the dining room table as a desk and a cardboard box as a file cabinet, the stress and strain of operating without proper space and supplies will take its toll.

- Have a separate room or area for your business, with a separate entrance if clients visit. Consider sound-proofing so your family won't be bothered by your noise and vice versa. In addition to the psychological and physical comfort of having a separate room for your home office, the IRS requires it in order for you to make a legitimate claim for tax deductions.

an agenda and a time limit. Even if you didn't call the meeting, if you see that it has no focus or structure you can step in and say, "I have another appointment in an hour. What topics do we have to cover in that hour? " then list those topics as the agenda.

One more time management tip: Use one of the popular time management planning systems to help you get the most out of your day. They include Day Timer (Day Timers, Inc., One Day-Timer Plaza, Allentown, PA 18195-1551; 800-225-5005), Day Runner (Harper House, Inc., available through stationery stores), and Planner Pad (Planner Pads, Inc., 5088 S. 107th St., Omaha, NE 68127; 402-592-0666). These and other systems give you a place to record appointments, daily to-do lists, special projects and their steps, as well as a contact book for names and addresses. If you spend most of your time in the office at a computer, there are numerous contact management and scheduling programs that will help you manage your time. If you use a portable computer, you can install these programs and carry this information wherever you go. A simple daily planner is illustrated in Figure 2.2 (on page 41).

ABC Travel Service

DAY OF THE WEEK:
Tuesday, 13th
MONTH AND YEAR:
Jun 1995

TIME	TO DO	NOTES
8:00 - 9:00	Pick up tickets at main office	Leave a note for Benjamin
9:00 - 10:00	Make confirmation callbacks with customers	
10:00 - 11:00	10:-10:30 - Staff meeting; meet new agent	
11:00 - 12:00	Plan Harper and Collins trips with itineraries	
12:00 - 1:00	Lunch with new agent	Stop by post office on way back
1:00 - 2:00	Return calls; talk with Jim about tour	
2:00 - 3:00	Confirmations	
3:00 - 4:00		
4:00 - 5:00	Call backs	
5:00 - 6:00		
6:00 - 7:00		
7:00 - 8:00	Get acquainted party with Nyler Tours	Ask about Tahiti fam
8:00 - 9:00		
9:00 - 10:00		
10:00 - 11:00		
11:00 - 12:00		

Figure 2.2: Efficient use of your time requires a daily planner.

Action Guidelines

You've learned the requirements of starting and operating a successful travel service. They include evaluating your personal and financial goals as well as your tolerance for risk; reviewing the tools you need; calculating financial requirements; assessing the skills you will need to be successful; and learning how to efficiently manage your time. Here's how to implement what you've learned in this chapter.

✔ Using your travel business notebook, make notes regarding your personal goals and values, your financial goals, and your tolerance for risk. Be as honest as possible.

✔ Plan your purchase of a computer, printer, and software for your travel service. Don't buy it yet; just start learning what you can about them.

✔ Start gathering your reference library.

✔ Complete the financial worksheet in this chapter to determine how much money you'll need and where you can get it.

✔ List the skills you'll need to enhance or add to make your travel service successful. How can you develop or improve on these skills?

✔ Select and use a time-management system if you don't already.

✔ Review your travel service requirements and start thinking about resources, the topic of the next chapter.

Chapter

3

RESOURCES FOR YOUR TRAVEL SERVICE

A resource is a person, product, or service that can help you with your objectives. Resources for your travel service include your own experiences, your prospective customers, trade associations, conventions, seminars, training courses, books, magazines, and governmental offices. Together they can increase your working knowledge of travel services and business, as well as help you understand how to work efficiently and profitably.

This chapter offers information on these and other resources. Included are addresses and telephone numbers when appropriate to help you get your travel service off the ground.

Reviewing Your Travel Experiences

The first and most important resource for your travel service is you. Your experiences with travel services may be limited to holiday flights to visit family. Or you may have experience in business travel or international travel. Or maybe you don't have extensive experience with travel services, but you do have a broad knowledge of geography and people, and a strong desire to work in the travel industry.

The point is that to serve your customers well you must understand their needs. You must know how they feel, what they need, how they buy, and how and why they travel. The best experience you can have is as someone with broad travel experience of your own as well as experience helping others solve their travel problems.

Take time to review your own experiences with travel and travel services. Have they been good or bad? What have you learned from them?

- Which of your own trips have been successful and which have not?

- Were there any specific destinations that you enjoyed most?

- If you are an experienced travel agent, what types of travel and customers do you prefer to work with?

- Did you discover a special hideaway you want to share with others?

- Do you have any special insights on travel or unique challenges you had to overcome to travel?

- List five or six elements that, in your experience, must be included in an effective travel service.

In any business, success requires empathy, and empathy requires experience. The more you understand about your customer, the better you will be able to serve him or her.

Discovering Your Customers' Needs

Gilbert K. Chesterton once said, "The traveler sees what he sees, the tourist sees what he has come to see."

The best way to understand your customers is to interview them. Find out what they are thinking. Understand what they want from a travel service and from you. Ask them what is most important to them. Learn what makes them select one travel service over another. Are they tourists or travelers? Which are you?

How can you find out what customers want before you start your travel service? By interviewing prospective customers. Talk with friends who have recently traveled, especially to destinations that you are considering representing. Set up a part-time travel service, such as on weekends, and interview people who respond to your ad.

In general, you'll learn that your customers want an effective travel service that understands and remembers the needs of the individual. They want personalized service. Depending on your chosen clientele, the next most important requirement may be price, speed, or quality. They may need to have a travel service that offers the lowest cruise fares or one that can arrange a business trip with six hours' notice. You may learn that two of these three elements—price, speed, quality—are already served in your area and that there is a sufficiently large market for travel services that are developed for the third element.

Chapter 6 will cover marketing in greater detail. For now, work toward an understanding of your potential customers' needs.

Trade Associations for Travel Agents

You're not alone. A trade association is a group of businesses that agree to share information among themselves regarding their trade. Plumbers have them, auto manufacturers have them; so do travel agents. There are numerous trade associations for travel agents and travel services, each with a specific purpose. Some serve as a clearinghouse for information on the travel industry. Others help those within a specific region or specialized type of travel.

The leading trading associations for this profession include:

- American Society of Travel Agents (1101 King St., Alexandria, VA 22314; 703-739-2782). ASTA is the largest trade association for travel agents and agencies with 20,000 members. It offers agency and associate membership, and requires dues.

- Association of Retail Travel Agents (1745 Jefferson Davis Hwy., Suite 300, Arlington, VA 22202; 703-413-2222). ARTA serves travel services that serve travelers from retail locations rather than homebased or inhouse travel agents.

- Alliance of Canadian Travel Associates (1729 Bank St., Suite 201, Ottawa, ON K1V 7Z5 CANADA; 612-521-0474). ACTA is Canada's association of travel agents.

- Cruise Lines International Association (500 Fifth Ave., Suite 1407, New York, NY 10110; 212-921-0066). CLIA serves the large cruise ship travel industry.

- National Association of Cruise-Only Agencies (3191 Coral Way, Suite 630, Miami, FL 33145; 305-446-

7732). NACOA specializes in helping travel agencies that only or primarily sell passage on cruise ships.

- Outside Sales Support Network (1061 E. Indiantown Rd., Suite 410, Jupiter, FL 33477; 407-575-7327). OSSN serves independent or outside travel agents who work under contract with one or more travel agencies.

- Travel Industry Association (TIA) (1133 21st St. NW, Suite 800, Washington, DC 20036; 202-293-1040).

- United States Tour Operators Association (USTOA), 211 E. 51st St., Suite 12B, New York, NY 10022; 212-750-7371).

- National Tour Association (NTA) (546 E. Main St., Lexington, KY 40508; 800-755-8687).

Airline Ticket Settlement

As mentioned earlier, to sell airline tickets you will need to have membership in one of two organizations. This is called settlement.

In the U.S., contact Airlines Reporting Corporation (P.O. Box 96194, Washington, DC 20090; 703-816-8000). ARC membership includes Area Settlement Plan (ASP) for collecting money from agencies and distributing payment to airlines. To sell airline tickets for most domestic air carriers, a travel agent must be approved by the ARC or work for an ARC-approved agency. Membership currently requires a bond or irrevocable letter of credit of $20,000. Other requirements include physical access by public at commercial premises and two or more experienced agents in the office at least 32 hours a week.

Here's how ARC settlement works: Once a week, you are sent a report of tickets purchased by your agency on behalf of your customers. The cost is then directly withdrawn from your business bank account by the ARC and deposited to the appropriate airline's account. The reporting week is Monday through Sunday.

International air carriers are members of International Airlines Travel Agent Network (300 Garden City Plaza, Suite 342, Garden City, NY 11530; 516-747-4716 or 2000 Peel St., Montreal, QB H3A 2R4 CANADA; 514-844-6311). IATAN membership is necessary for ticketing many international air carriers.

Your travel service must either be a member of the respective group or contract with a travel agency that is a member in order to sell and print tickets for domestic and international flights. Opportunities for contracting with a member agency are explained later in this chapter under "Instant Travel Services."

Certification Programs

Nearly every industry has a certification program to maintain professional standards as well as give the consumer confidence in the trade. Institute of Certified Travel Agents (148 Linden St., Wellesley, MA 02181; 617-237-0280) does so for travel agents. The ICTA authorizes the title of Certified Travel Counselor to those who complete training in travel agency management as well as in the travel industry. ICTA also offers courses and training toward certification.

Conventions and Seminars

Many professional associations and marketing groups sponsor annual conventions of members and professionals. Workshops, guest speakers, and roundtables are organized to encourage travel agents from across the country to share information, techniques, and ideas. Here are a few of the conventions and seminars for travel agents.

- ASTA World Travel Congress (American Society of Travel Agents, 1101 King St., Alexandria, VA 22314; 703-739-2782). The 1994 convention was in Lisbon.

- ARTA Conference and Exhibition (Association of Retail Travel Agents, 1745 Jefferson Davis Hwy., Suite 300, Arlington, VA 22202; 703-413-2222). For those who own and work for retail travel agencies.
- NACOA Convention (National Association of Cruise-Only Agencies, 3191 Coral Way, Suite 630, Miami, FL 33145; 305-446-7732). For cruise-only travel services.

Magazines and Trade Journals

There are dozens of magazines for travel comsumers and professionals. Besides those found on larger magazine racks, they include:

- *ASTA Agency Management* (1301 Carolina St., Greensboro, NC 27401; 800-828-2712)
- *Business Travel News* (600 Community Dr., Manhasset, NY 11030; 516-365-4600)
- *Tour and Travel News* (600 Community Dr., Manhasset, NY 11030; 516-562-5000)
- *Travel Agent* (801 Second Ave., New York, NY 10017; 212-370-5050)
- *Travel Weekly* (500 Plaza Drive, Secaucus, NJ 07094; 201-902-1500)

Instant Travel Services

There are four ways you can go into business:

- On your own
- Buy an existing business
- Buy a business opportunity package
- Buy a franchise

Starting out on your own is least expensive. Buy a practical book (like this one), follow the instructions, add some imagination, and start your business. Buying an existing business is a good option if you have sufficient capital. Buying a business opportunity package gives you the experience of a successful business without all of the costs of buying the business. A franchise gives you not only the tools to start your business, but a proven name as well.

What does an established travel service cost? Typically, about 10 percent of gross sales. That is, a travel service that is billing $1 million a year will cost about $100,000 to buy. If the business is shrinking, you may be able to purchase it for 8 percent of gross sales. Expect to pay about 25 percent down, with the balance paid out over two to five years.

A business opportunity gives you guidelines, some training, some tools, and a push-start. Typical initial investment for a travel service opportunity is $5,000 to $10,000. A monthly or annual fee will probably be assessed, based on how much you make or some other factor. A few let you work as an outside agent for their travel service, splitting the commissions. You will receive 40-80 percent of the commission, depending on what is sold and your agreement with the business opportunity provider. Travel service business opportunities include:

- Buckingham Travel Group (604 Brazos St., Austin, TX 78701; 512-472-3099). Buckingham's opportunity includes computer, software, training, books, and supplies.

- Eagle Travel Marketing (4449 Astor Dr., Lake Worth, FL 33461; 800-993-0005). Eagle's package includes commercial SABRE, reference books, training, telephone support and backup staff.

- Leisure Resource (344 W. Main St., Milford, CT 06460; 800-729-9051). They use outside agents, requiring a small setup fee and offering a commission.

Franchising is a form of licensing by which the owner (the franchisor) of a product or service distributes through affiliated dealers (the franchisees). The franchise license is typically for a specific geographical area. The product or service is marketed by a brand name (McDonalds, Thomas Cook), and the franchisor controls the way that it is marketed. The franchisor requires consistency among the franchisees: standardized products or services, trademarks, uniform symbols, equipment, and storefronts. The franchisor typically offers assistance in organizing, training, merchandising, and management. In exchange, the franchisor receives initial franchise fees and an ongoing fee based on sales levels. Franchises in the travel service business include:

- Ask Mr. Foster Associates (7833 Haskell Ave., Van Nuys, CA 91406)
- Cruise Holidays International (4740 Murphy Canyon Rd., Suite 200, San Diego, CA 92123)
- Cruise of a Lifetime (237 Park Ave., 21st Floor, New York, NY 10017)
- Cruise Shoppes America (115 Metairie Rd., Suite E, Metairie, LA 70005)
- Cruises Only (100 First St., Suite 105, Pittsburgh, PA 15222)
- Empress Travel Franchise (450 Harmon Meadow Blvd., Secaucus, NJ 07096)
- Fugazy International (555 Madison Ave., New York, NY 10022)
- Hartley Vacation Centers (508 Reservoir Ave., Cranston, RI 02910)
- International Tours (2840 E. 51st St., 2nd Floor, Tulsa, OK 74105)
- Travelhost Agencies (8080 N. Central Expressway, 14th Floor, Dallas, TX 75206)

- Travel Agents International (111 Second Ave. NE, 15th Floor, St. Petersburg, FL 33731)
- Travelplex International (655 Metro Pl. S., Suite 250, Dublin, OH 43017)
- Travel Professionals International (10172 Linn Station Rd., Suite 360, Louisville, KY 40223)
- Travel Franchise System (4350 La Jolla Village Dr., San Diego, CA 92122)
- Uniglobe Travel (1199 W. Pender St., Suite 900, Vancouver, BC V6E 2R1 CANADA).

One useful source of information on available franchises is the *Franchise Opportunities Handbook* produced and published by the United States Department of Commerce and available through the Superintendent of Documents (U.S. Government Printing Office, Washington, DC 20402) or your regional federal bookstore. This handbook lists basic information on franchises available in 44 categories including: the name and address of the franchisor, a description of the operation, number of franchises, how long the franchise has been in business, how much equity capital is needed, how much financial assistance is available, what training is provided, and what managerial assistance is available.

Another source of information on franchises is the International Franchise Association (1350 New York Avenue N.W., Suite 900, Washington, DC 20005). The IFA's *Franchise Opportunities Guide* is a comprehensive listing of franchisors by industry and business category. *Franchising Opportunities* is their bimonthly magazine. Their newsletter, *Franchising World*, includes information on developing trends in franchising.

Other sources include *Entrepreneur, Income Opportunities*, and other magazines available on most newsstands.

In addition to franchises are business opportunities and resource suppliers. A business opportunity allows you to sell their product or service without the strict requirements of a franchise. Depending on the opportunity, you may be licensed to use their name in your advertisement. A supplier will furnish you with a product that you can then resell to your customers.

Small Business Administration Resources

Founded more than 40 years ago, the U.S. Small Business Administration or SBA (1441 L Street N.W., Washington, DC 20416) has offices in 100 cities across the U.S. and a charter to help small businesses start and grow. The SBA offers counseling, booklets on business topics, and administers a small business loan guarantee program. To find your area's SBA office, check the White Pages of metropolitan telephone books in your region under "United States Government, Small Business Administration."

The SBA also operates the Small Business Answer Desk, a toll-free response line (800-827-5722) that answers questions about SBA services. In addition, it sponsors the 13,000 Service Corps of Retired Executives (SCORE) volunteers, Active Corps of Executives (ACE) volunteers, Business Development Centers, and Technology Access Centers.

The SBA offers numerous publications, services, and videos for starting and managing small businesses. Publications are available on products/ideas/inventions, financial management, management and planning, marketing, crime prevention, personnel management, and other topics. The booklets can be purchased for one or two dollars each at SBA offices or from SBA Publications, P.O. Box 30, Denver, CO 80201. Ask first for SBA Form 115A, The Small Business Directory, that lists available publications and includes an order form.

Another popular service is SBA On-Line, a computer bulletin board operated by the Small Business Administration. It receives more than 1,000 calls a day and has handled one million calls since it opened in 1992. Once you're familiar with computers and modems, you can access this resource by having your system call 900-463-4636. There is a small fee for its use, currently about $6 an hour. The bulletin board includes extensive resources for small businesses and access to other government agencies. If you want to access a limited version of this popular bulletin board, dial 800-697-4636. It doesn't have as many resources, but it is free.

The Service Corps of Retired Executives (SCORE; 1441 L Street N.W./Room 100, Washington, DC 20416) is a national non-profit association with a goal of helping small business. SCORE is sponsored by the SBA and the local office is usually in or near that of the local SBA office. SCORE members, retired men and women, and ACE members, still active in their own business, donate their time and experience to counseling individuals regarding small business.

The 700 Business Development Centers (BDCs) are regional centers funded by the SBA and managed in conjunction with regional colleges. A BDC offers free and confidential counseling for small business owners and managers, new businesses, home-based businesses, and people with ideas concerning retail, service, wholesale, manufacturing, and farm businesses. BDCs sponsor seminars on various business topics, assist in developing business and marketing plans, inform entrepreneurs of employer requirements, and teach cash flow budgeting and management. BDCs also gather information sources, assist in locating business resources, and make referrals.

Small Business Institutes are partnerships between the SBA and nearly 500 colleges offering counseling services to area businesses. SBIs conduct market research, develop business and marketing plans, and help small businesses work out manufacturing problems. Contact your regional SBA office to find out if a local college has such a program. You could get free or low-cost assistance from the college's business faculty and students.

Tax Information Resources

The U.S. Treasury Department's Internal Revenue Service offers numerous Small Business Tax Education Program videos through their regional offices. Topics include depreciation, business use of your home, employment taxes, excise taxes, starting a business, sole proprietorships, partnerships, self-employed retirement plans, Sub-Chapter S corporations, and federal tax deposits.

If you're considering using a portion of your home as a business office, request *Business Use of Your Home* (Publication 587) from the Internal Revenue Service (Washington, DC 20224). It's free and will help you determine if your business qualifies for this option as well as how to take advantage of it to lower your taxes.

Depending on how much you use your business vehicle for personal use, you can either list all costs of operating the vehicle as an expense or you can deduct a standard mileage rate as an expense when you file income taxes. For more information, request *Business Use of a Car* (Publication 917) from the Internal Revenue Service. There's no charge for this publication. Figure 3.1, on page 56, is a worksheet for calculating your business mileage deduction.

What business expenses are deductible? There's a long list. The best answer is found in a free publication offered by the Internal Revenue Service, *Business Expenses* (Publication 535).

ABC Travel Service

AUTOMOBILE TRAVEL LOG

Monthly Summary Sheet

Date:

AUTOMOBILE INFORMATION

Make of Auto: Honda LX

Year & Model: 1993

Vehicle I.D. Number: 1234567890

Driver of Vehicle: Barbara Simmons

Odometer   End of month: 12,345.00

Beginning of month: 11,111.00

Total Miles Driven: 1,234.00

Qualified Business Miles Driven: 1,234.00

Allowable Reimbursement Rate: 1,234.00   x $ 0.28 /mi

Total Expense $ $345.52

YEAR TO DATE - INFORMATION

	BUSINESS MILES	TOTAL MILES
Prior YTD	5,678	5,678
Current Month	1,234	1,234
New YTD	6,912	6,912

DATE: 　　　　　SIGNATURE :

APPROVAL :

Figure 3.1: Automotive mileage driven for business purposes is a legitimate expense. Keep track of mileage with a travel log, such as this one.

Action Guidelines

There is a wide variety of resources available to professional travel agents including your experiences, prospective customers, trade associations, conventions, seminars, training courses, books, magazines, suppliers, and governmental offices. Here's how to put them to work for you.

✔ Review your own experiences with travel services as well as the experiences of friends and family.

✔ Make notes in your travel business notebook on what you feel your prospective customers need and want from a travel service.

✔ Start calling and writing for catalogs and information from resources.

✔ Review your list of skills and needs then find training resources to enhance them.

✔ Contact franchisors to determine costs and benefits of buying a franchise or opportunity.

✔ Contact your regional SBA and BDC offices to learn how they can help you start and build your business.

✔ Contact the IRS for booklets, forms, and other resources.

Chapter

4

STARTING YOUR TRAVEL SERVICE

B y now, you've learned what a successful travel service does, studied the resources available to you, and decided that you want to start your own travel business. You're ready to put your sign out and find your first client.

Not yet. Before you start your travel service you must first plan to make it a success. You don't want to close up shop in six months because you misjudged the local market or overspent your income. Instead, you want to celebrate your first anniversary looking back on a successful year and looking forward to many more.

This chapter will help you plan for your success, then execute that plan to ensure that your travel business will be profitable.

Starting a Successful Travel Service

The adage that businesses don't plan to fail, they just fail to plan is accurate. Without a plan for your business, you may soon find yourself in a venture that neither satisfies your needs nor pays your bills.

A business plan is a document that can be used both by people contemplating going into business and those already in business. A business plan helps you focus your thoughts and ideas, summarizing your product, your process, your market, and your expectations into a single document that can guide you in your daily decisions as well as help you develop financing for start-up and expansion.

An excellent guide for creating a successful business plan is David H. Bangs Jr.'s best-seller *The Business Planning Guide, Sixth Edition* (Upstart Publishing). It offers clear, step-by-step procedures for pulling a business plan together for a travel service or any other business venture. It includes worksheets, resources, and a sample business plan.

Your business plan will answer these five questions:

1. How much money do I need?
2. On what will the money be spent?
3. Who will own and who will operate the business?
4. What are the projected financial results of the business?
5. Do I really know enough about this business?

If your business plan is intended to develop financing through a bank or a backer, it must also answer the question: How will the funds be repaid?

Your business plan will include a statement of purpose, an outline of your product or service, a discussion of your customers and how you will reach them, as well as current and projected financial information.

A typical travel service may develop a statement of purpose that reads:

> ABC Travel Service will offer cost-effective vacation travel service for families in the Clemmings Shopping Center area. Start-up requires $10,000 in cash from savings for equipment, rent, supplies, and a salary for the first two months of operation until the business is expected to be profitable.

If you're using the business plan to develop financing, it will be more developed and specific than the plan you would write to guide you through the first year of operation. In addition, a business plan for a $10,000 start-up is typically shorter than one for a $100,000 expansion project.

Selecting Your Business Name

Naming a business is much like naming a baby. In some ways, it will give direction to its growth. A well-named business will seem more successful to prospects and will then become so.

A business name should make it clear to prospects what the firm does, or at least the industry the firm is in. Here are some examples:

- Midtown Travel Service (describes the location and the product)
- Sandra's Travel Service (identifies the product, but is personalized at the expense of sounding like a small business)
- Henderson Travel Services, Inc. (sounds bigger; surnames are better than first names and Inc. implies that it is a larger firm—but can be used only if your business is incorporated)
- ABC Travel Service (specifically identifies the service and assures first-listing in alphabetical directories such as telephone Yellow Pages)

- Smithtown Services (unclear what service is involved)
- High Adventure Travel (clearly identifies the product)

In selecting a business name, many firms write a defining motto or slogan (Figure 4.1, on page 63) that's used in all stationery and advertisements to further clarify what the firm does:

- Specializing in travel services for senior citizens
- Specializing in low-cost travel to the Mexican Riviera
- Plan to have fun with us!
- Helping you get the most from your travel dollar
- Serving the business traveler
- Timeless travel since 1975
- Your One-Stop Travel Service

An assumed business name is a name other than the real and true name of each person operating a business. A real and true name becomes an assumed business name with the addition of any words that imply the existence of additional owners. For example, Bob Smith is a real and true name, while Bob Smith Company is an assumed business name.

In most states and counties, you must register an assumed business name (d.b.a. or "doing business as") to let the public know who is transacting business under that name. Without the registration you may be fined or, worse, not be able to defend a legal action because your assumed business name wasn't properly registered. Most assumed business name registrations also require a fee, which is usually small.

In many states, an assumed business name is registered with the state's corporate division. Some states will also register your assumed business name with counties in which you do business. Other states require that you do so. In some locations, you must publish a public notice in an area newspaper

Figure 4.1: Your business logo can effectively communicate your image to prospects and customers.

telling all that you (and any other business principals) are operating under a specific business name.

The typical assumed business name registration requires the following information: the business name you wish to assume, the principal place of business, the name of an authorized representative, your SIC code (standard industrial classification; for a travel agency or bureau it is 4724-02), a list of all owners with their signatures, and a list of all counties in which your firm will transact business (sell, lease, or purchase goods or services; receive funding or credit).

Locating Your Travel Service

Where will you locate your travel service? The answer depends on how much business you expect to initially earn, what your space requirements are, your budget, and whether you plan to have clients visit your place of business.

Here are some points to consider as you decide where to locate your business:

- Proximity to your primary clients
- Opportunities for signage

- Availability of transportation
- Requirements and availability of parking facilities
- Cost of operation
- Tax burden
- Quality of police and fire services
- Environmental factors
- Physical suitability of building
- Opportunities for future expansion
- Personal convenience

The first and most important consideration is making sure that you are located conveniently for your clients. The best locations for travel services are near colleges, universities, trade schools, business schools, employment offices, or in major business districts, depending on your primary clientele. Considering these factors, let's look at your options.

Home Office

Approximately 30 percent of all travel services operate exclusively from someone's home. The majority are independent contractors or outside agents for larger travel agencies. Some start at home and move to business offices as they grow. The entrepreneur sets up a small office at the dining table, in a walk-in closet, an extra bedroom, or a shop. This is an ideal situation for a part-time travel service for many reasons. First, there will be little or no additional rent expense. It is also more convenient for you to have all your records at home, where you can review them at any time. In addition, you could ask a family member or someone living with you to answer the telephone while you're away. Finally, you can legally deduct some of your household costs as legitimate expenses and reduce your tax obligation.

But the best reason is that it saves you time. A client can call you in the evening to ask about a specific trip and you can quickly check your records or make notes in their file without leaving your home. The most popular initial location for a home-based travel service is a desk in a spare room.

Of course, with a home office you will want to discourage walk-in customers. Don't include your address in your ads. Rather, have prospects call you to set up an appointment. Make sure that the path from your front door to your office is short and looks as professional as possible. Customers are hiring you for your professionalism as well as your travel knowledge.

Remember, though, operating a travel service from your home is typically only temporary and only for part-time businesses. Once you've developed a clientele and are ready to make your business full-time, seriously consider a commercial location.

Your Own Office

As your travel service business grows, you will want to move to your own office. The biggest disadvantage of such a move is the cost. But there are many advantages. First, your own office will give you an image of being a large, successful, and permanent firm. Second, your business requires that prospects, clients, or others come to your office. An office of your own will give them a better first impression. Third, it will give you control over your business that you cannot have if you're working out of a spare bedroom or a shared office.

Many travel services prefer to locate in professional office centers with other services that serve the business community: attorneys, employment agencies, copy shops, desktop publishing services. Especially consider professional office centers that have well-known clients that will encourage foot traffic.

Shopping Mall

Travel services that locate in storefronts or shopping malls are called retail agencies. They sell a product and service just as any other business would. A great benefit of starting a retail agency in a storefront or shopping mall is visibility. People going for a dress, a haircut, or a hot dog see your signs.

Remember, though, that a retail travel service in a shopping mall may be required to be open seven days a week.

Travel services typically don't locate in a shopping mall because of the high costs. However, many take advantage of the mall's traffic by renting a professional office on a mall's second floor or in a satellite office complex next to a popular mall. There are many types of shopping malls: neighborhood, community, regional, and super-regional.

A neighborhood shopping center is built around a supermarket or drugstore with a trade population of 2,500 to 40,000 and offers 30,000 to 100,000 square feet of leasable space.

A community shopping center (100,000 to 300,000 square feet) often has a variety or discount department store as its leading tenant and serves a trade population of 40,000 to 150,000.

A regional shopping center (300,000 to 1,000,000 square feet) builds around one or more full-line department stores with a trade population of 150,000 or more.

A super-regional shopping center includes three or more department stores with more than 750,000 square feet of leasable space.

Selecting a Location

As mentioned, the most important factor in selecting a retail location is retail compatibility. For your small business in its early years of operation, with limited funds for advertising and promotion, locating near a traffic-generator can help you survive. You'll often find restaurants grouped together. Competing antique stores may take over a city block. The old business adage says that the three most important factors in selecting a retail site are: location, location, and location.

The next most important factor in selecting your retail site is the availability of a local merchants association. A strong merchants association can accomplish through group strength what an individual store owner couldn't even dream of. A merchants association cannot only speak as a booming voice to city planners, but also bulk-buy advertising at lower rates and promote its own events. But make sure that you understand your responsibilities to the association before you sign up. If the site you select doesn't have a merchants association, consider starting one.

Other factors include the responsiveness of the landlord and the opportunities for negotiating a favorable lease. Make sure your new landlord is continuing to invest in the property, including regular maintenance and quick repairs. And talk with other commercial landlords in your area to ensure that your lease is the best you can negotiate.

You can often get assistance on selecting a retail site by talking with local and regional chambers of commerce about your needs. They may be able to give you an educated guess on what you will probably have to pay for a property that will help your business become successful.

Zoning Laws

Your travel business location may be limited by local zoning laws. Before deciding where you will set up your business, talk to the local zoning office about restrictions. You may find that so-called cottage or home businesses are allowed in your neighborhood as long as clients don't park on the street.

The Americans with Disabilities Act (ADA) requires that business owners offer access to their location that does not restrict employees or customers with disabilities. This act applies to all businesses with 15 or more employees.

Employment Laws You Must Know About

Before you hire your first employee, know that there are certain laws, federal and state, that come into play. Your local state employment office can assist you in learning the current requirements of these laws.

- The Social Security Act of 1935, as amended, is concerned with employment insurance laws as well as retirement insurance.

- The Fair Labor Standards Act of 1938, as amended, establishes minimum wages, overtime pay, record keeping, and child labor standards for most businesses.

- The Occupational Safety and Health Act (OSHA) of 1970 is concerned with safety and health in the workplace and covers almost all employers. There are specific standards, regulations, and reporting requirements that must be met.

There are other laws that may concern your business. Contact your local state employment office to determine the requirements for hiring disadvantaged workers, federal service contracts for work on public buildings or other public projects, employee pension and welfare benefit plans, and the garnishment of an employee's wages.

In addition, the Immigration Reform and Control Act of 1986 prohibits employing illegal aliens. Employers must require every employee to fill out the Employment Eligibility Verification Form (Form 19) within three days of the date of hire (if hired after November 7, 1987). Fines are levied for noncompliance. For more information, contact the nearest office of the Immigration and Naturalization Service.

The Civil Rights Act of 1964 prohibits discrimination in employment practices because of race, religion, sex, or national origin. Public Law 90-202 prohibits discrimination on the basis of age with respect to individuals who are between 40 and 70 years of age. Federal laws also prohibit discrimination against the physically handicapped. Again, your state employment office can help you in understanding the laws regarding applicants and employment. In addition, firms like G. Neil (720 International Parkway, Sunrise, FL 33345) offer catalogs of human relations supplies: job applications, personnel folders, labor law posters, attendance controllers, employee awards, and related materials.

Figures 4.2 (on page 70) and 4.3 (on page 71) illustrate a typical job application form used by small businesses.

Forms of Business

One of the most important decisions you will make as you start your travel service business is what legal form it will take. Why so important? Because how you record expenses, how you build your business, how you pay taxes, how you treat profits, and how you manage liability all depend on the structure you give your business.

Of course, as your business grows, you'll be able to move from one type of structure to another, but sometimes there will be a cost. The cost will be paid to the tax man as he decides whether you changed structure to avoid paying your fair share of taxes. One of the reasons you may later change structure is because you want to legally reduce tax liability—and that's okay. It's the abuse of tax laws that brings the wrath of the IRS.

ABC Travel Service

JOB APPLICATION

Date:

Social Security Number

Name: _____ **Telephone:** _____
LAST   FIRST   INITIAL
Address: _____
STREET

CITY   STATE   ZIP

Education History

Institution	Name & Location	Grade Completed: Diploma/ Degree
High School		
University / College		
Other (Day / Night)		

Employment History (most current first)

Employer :		Your Job Title:
Address :		Duties:
		Reason for Leaving:
Phone:		Salary:
		Employment from : to:
Employer:		Your Job Title:
Address:		Duties:
		Reason for Leaving:
Phone:		Salary:
		Employment from : to:
Employer:		Your Job Title:
Address:		Duties:
		Reason for Leaving:
Phone:		Salary:
		Employment from : to:

JOB APPLICATION Page 1.

Figure 4.2: A typical job application form gathers information on education and employment history.

References

	Name	Occupation	Telephone
1			
2			
3			

Skills

○　　　　　　　　　　　○
○　　　　　　　　　　　○
○　　　　　　　　　　　○
○　　　　　　　　　　　○
○　　　　　　　　　　　○ Other explain:

Date Available	Position Applied For:
Hours Available	Shift Desired:　☐ Day ☐ Night
Salary Expected	☐ Afternoon ☐ Any Shift

The information provided on this application is accurate to the best of my knowledge and subject to verification by this company. I understand that proof of age may be required upon employment. I understand I must truthfully answer all the questions on this application. I also understand that if I do not, I may be refused employment, or separated if I am a current company employee. While employed by this company I agree not to engage in any other business or employment without the consent of this company.

If employment results from this application, I understand that additional personal data or a physical examination may be required if I am eligible for benefits.
I authorize all previous employers to furnish this company with any information they may have regarding my employment and my reason for leaving, and I release my prior employers and this company from all liability for and damage resulting from the information provided.
I fully understand that if I am not bondable by a surety company, this company may be unable to offer employment.

SIGNATURE: _____　　*DATE:* _____

FOR INTERNAL USE ONLY

INTERVIEWER _____　　| DATE |

COMMENTS
_____
_____
_____
_____
_____

Accepted ○　　　Not Accepted ○

JOB APPLICATION Page 2.

Figure 4.3:　A job application form also records information on references, skills, and position applied for. It is useful to have a place for your comments, which you can write during or directly after the interviewing.

There are four common types of business structures: proprietorship, partnership, corporation and, a relatively new structure, the limited liability company. Each has specific advantages and disadvantages, but they must all be considered against your individual circumstances, goals, and needs.

Proprietorship

A sole proprietorship is a business that is owned and operated by one person. However, in many states a business owned jointly by a husband and wife is considered a proprietorship rather than a partnership. This is the easiest form of business to establish. You only need to obtain required licenses and begin operation. For its simplicity, the proprietorship is the most widespread form of small business organization and is especially popular with the new travel agent.

The first and most obvious advantage of a proprietorship is ease of formation. There is less formality and fewer legal restrictions associated with establishing a sole proprietorship. It needs little or no governmental approval and is less expensive to start than a partnership or a corporation.

Another advantage of a proprietorship is that it doesn't require that you share profits with anyone. Whatever is left over after you pay the bills (including the tax man) is yours to keep. You will report income, expenses, and profit to the IRS using Schedule C and your standard 1040 form, and make quarterly estimated tax payments to the IRS so you don't get behind before your annual filing.

Control is important to the successful travel business. A proprietorship gives that control and decision-making power to a single person, you. Proprietorships also give the owner flexibility that other forms of business do not. A partner must usually get agreement from other partners. In larger matters, a corporation must get agreement from other members of the board of directors or corporate officers. A proprietor simply makes up his or her mind and acts.

One more plus: the sole proprietor has relative freedom from government control and special taxation. Sure, the government has some say in how you operate and what taxes you will pay. But the government has less to say to the sole proprietor.

Yes, there's a downside to being the only boss. Most important is unlimited liability. That is, the individual proprietor is responsible for the full amount of business debts, which may exceed the proprietor's total investment. With some exceptions, this liability extends to all the proprietor's assets, such as house and car. One way around this is for the proprietor to obtain sufficient insurance coverage to reduce the risk from physical loss and personal injury. But if your suppliers aren't getting paid, they can come after your personal assets.

When the business is a single individual, the serious illness or death of that person can end the business.

Individuals typically cannot get the credit and capital that partnerships and corporations can. Fortunately, most travel services don't require extensive capital. But when they do, they seriously consider the advantages of taking on a partner or becoming a corporation.

Finally, as a sole proprietor you have a relatively limited viewpoint and experience because you're only one person. You're more subject to tunnel vision or seeing things in a narrow way based on your experiences. You don't have someone with a commitment to your business who can give you a fresh viewpoint or new ideas.

Partnership

"The man who goes out alone can start today; but he who travels with another must wait till that other is ready." Henry

David Thoreau's words are true of travel. They are also true of business partnerships.

The Uniform Partnership Act (UPA) adopted by many states defines a partnership as "an association of two or more persons to carry on as co-owners of a business for profit." How the partnership is structured, the powers and limitations of each partner, and their participation in the business are written into a document called the Articles of Partnership. The articles or descriptions can either be written by the partners, found in a legal form from a stationery store, or written by an attorney. Obviously, using an attorney is the best option because it will ensure that the document is binding and reduce disputes that typically come up once the business is growing.

A partnership can typically raise capital more easily than a proprietorship. This is because there are more people whose assets can be combined as equity for the loan. Lenders will look at the credit ratings of each partner, so make sure that your business partners have good credit.

Partnerships are frequently more flexible in the decision-making process than a corporation, but less flexible than a proprietorship.

Like proprietorships, partnerships offer relative freedom from government control and special taxation. A partnership doesn't pay income tax. Rather, all profits and losses flow through the partnership to the individual partners who pay income and other taxes as if they were sole proprietors.

Of course, there are some minuses to partnerships. Like sole proprietorships, at least one partner will be a *general partner* and will assume unlimited liability for the business. It is wise to obtain sufficient insurance coverage to reduce the risk of loss from physical loss or personal injury, but the general partner is still liable.

A partnership is as stable or as unstable as its members. Elimination of any partner often means automatic dissolution of the partnership. However, the business can continue to

Your firm's Articles of Partnership should include:

- the name, location, length, and purpose of the partnership,
- the type of partnership,
- a definition of the partners' individual contributions,
- an agreement on how business expenses will be handled,
- an outline of the authority of each partner,
- a summary of the accounting methods that will be used,
- a definition of how profits and losses will be distributed among the partners,
- the salaries and capital draws for each partner,
- an agreement of how the partnership will be modified or terminated, including dissolution of the partnership by death or disability of a member or by the decision of partners to disband, and
- a description of how the members will arbitrate and settle disputes as well as change terms of the partnership agreement.

Partnerships are easier and less costly to form than corporations. In most states, all that's really needed is Articles of Partnership.

operate if the agreement includes provisions for the right of survivorship and possible creation of a new partnership. Partnership insurance can assist surviving partners in purchasing the equity of a deceased partner.

Though a partnership has less difficulty in getting financing than a sole proprietorship, the fragile nature of partnerships sometimes makes it difficult to get long-term financing. The best source is using the combined equity of the partners from assets they own as individuals. In fact, many partnerships are started because an active partner needs equity or financing that he cannot get without a partner with more assets or better credit.

Depending upon how the partnership agreement is drawn up, any partner may be able to bind all of the partners to financial obligations. Make sure your Articles of Partnership accurately reflects your intent regarding how partners can or cannot obligate the partnership. Also consider the advantages and disadvantages of structuring your partnership as a limited liability company, discussed in this book right after corporations.

A major drawback to partnerships is the difficulty faced when arranging the leaving of a partner. Buying out the partner's interest may be difficult unless terms have been specifically worked out in the partnership agreement.

As you can see, there are numerous pluses and minuses to partnerships. Many of the disadvantages can be addressed in your Articles of Partnership. This is why it is recommended that you use an attorney experienced in such agreements as you construct your partnership. The cost is usually less than the value.

Corporation

About two-thirds of all travel agencies incorporate. Why? Primarily for liability reasons. Businesses, as they grow, often become corporations, identified by an extension to their name: Corp., Inc., or, in Canada, Ltd. A corporation (called a C corporation) is usually formed by the authority of a state government. The steps to forming a corporation begin with writing incorporation papers and issuing capital stock. Then, approval must be obtained from the secretary of state in the state in which the corporation is being formed. Only then can the corporation act as a legal entity separate from those who own its stock.

The primary advantage to incorporation is that it limits the stockholder's liability to their investment. If you buy $1,000 of stock in a corporation and it fails, you can only lose up to the $1,000 investment. The corporation's creditors cannot come back to you demanding more money. The exception is when you put up some of your own assets as collateral for the corporation.

Ownership of a corporation is a transferable asset. In fact, the New York Stock Exchange and other exchanges make a big business out of transferring stock, or partial ownership, in corporations from one investor to another. If your travel service business is a corporation, you can sell partial ownership or stock in it within certain limits. In fact, this is how many corporations get money to grow. A corporation can also issue long-term bonds to gain cash required to purchase assets or build the business.

Your corporation has a separate and legal existence. Your corporation is not you or anybody else. It is itself. For example, in the case of illness, death, or other cause for loss of a corporate officer or owner, the corporation continues to exist and do business.

The corporation can also delegate authority to hired managers, although they are often one and the same. Thus you become an employee of the corporation.

Corporations have disadvantages, too. The corporation's state charter may limit the type of business it does to a specific industry or service. However, other states allow broad charters that permit corporations to operate in any legal enterprise.

Corporations face more governmental regulations on all levels: local, state, and federal. That means your business will spend more time and money fulfilling these requirements as a corporation than it would as a proprietorship or a partnership.

If your corporate manager is not also a stockholder, he will have less incentive to be efficient than he would if he had a share in your business.

As you can imagine, a corporation is more expensive to form than other types of businesses. Even if you don't use an attorney, there are forms and fees that will quickly add up. However, an attorney is a good investment when incorporating your travel service business.

Finally, corporations allow the federal and some state governments to tax income twice: once as corporate net income and once as it's received by the individual stockholders in the form of salary or dividends. A Sub-Chapter S corporation allows small businesses to tax the business as if it were a sole proprietorship or partnership (no corporate income tax) and pass the tax liability on to the individual stockholders. There are about 1.6 million Sub-Chapter S corporations in the U.S. Recent changes in the law may make it easier to get financing for a Sub-S. Talk with an attorney or accountant about this option.

Limited Liability Company

Similar to a partnership, a limited liability company (LLC) is taxed only once on its profits. A C corporation, as mentioned, is taxed twice. Unlike a partnership, an LLC protects partners by limiting their personal liability for actions of the company. An LLC offers liability protections similar to a corporation. In addition, LLCs have fewer restrictions on shareholders and allow the transfer of shares more easily than a corporation.

Finally, profits are reported on personal rather than corporate tax returns.

LLCs must be privately held companies. While restructuring a C corporation into an LLC can be difficult and costly, changing your business from an LLC to a C corporation is quite easy. One major drawback to LLCs is that their limitation of liability has not been extensively tested in the court system, as it has with corporations. If you decide to establish an LLC, make sure you have an attorney who has experience with this structure and who can advise you based on liability and tax issues in your state.

About 40 states recognize limited liability companies as a legal business structure. They have been popular in other countries for many years. In establishing an LLC you will need to file articles of organization and an operating agreement with state authorities. For more information on LLCs, contact the Association of Limited Liability Companies (202-965-6565). *A Guide to Limited Liability Companies* is available from Commerce Clearing House (800-835-5224).

How to Hire an Attorney

To find an attorney who is familiar with business of your size and trade, ask for a referral from a business colleague, your banker, your accountant, your local chamber of commerce, or other business services in your area. Many local bar associations run an attorney referral and information service; check your local telephone book's Yellow Pages under "Attorneys' Referral & Information Services." Some referral services give you only names and phone numbers; others actually give information on experience and fees to help you match your needs to the attorney's background and charges.

An attorney can help you decide which is the most advan-
tageous business structure for you. He or she can also help you
with zoning, licensing problems, unpaid bills, contracts and
agreements, employment laws, copyright questions, trademarks, and some tax problems.

Because there is always the possibility of a lawsuit, claim, or
other legal action against your business, it is wise to have an
attorney who is already familiar with your business lined up
before a crisis arises. An attorney with experience serving
employment service businesses can also advise you on federal,
state, and local laws, programs, and agencies to help you prepare for or prevent potential problems.

Let your attorney know that you expect to be informed of
all developments and consulted before any decisions are made
on your behalf. You may also want to receive copies of all documents, letters, and memos written and received regarding
your project. If this isn't practical, you should at least have the
opportunity to read such correspondence at your attorney's
office.

How to Hire an Accountant

Many new travel services fail because of poor financial management. Sometimes the best decision a new business owner
makes is to hire the services of a public accounting firm. An
accountant can design record-keeping systems, set up ways for
maintaining records, analyze financial information, and help
you relate that information to profitability.

Daily bits of information will flow into your travel service
business. As you serve customers, you will generate information about sales, cash, supplies, purchase expenses, payroll,
accounts payable, and, if credit is offered to customers,
accounts receivable.

To capture these facts and figures, a system is necessary. If
you don't feel comfortable with setting up and managing such

a system, don't be shy about hiring an accounting service. An accountant can help design one for recording the information that you need to control finances and make profitable decisions.

Once a system of records has been set up, the question is: Who should keep the books? The accounting service who has set up the books may keep them. However, if you have a general understanding of record keeping you can do them yourself and save some money. Use your accountant for checking and analyzing your records. Once your business has grown, you may want to hire someone to keep your records and perform other office functions.

In addition to record keeping, an accountant can advise you on financial management, providing you with cash flow requirements, budget forecasts, borrowing, business organization, and tax information.

By analyzing cash flow requirements, an accountant can help you work out the amount of cash needed to operate your firm during a specific period—for example, three months, six months, the next year. He or she considers how much cash you will need to carry customer accounts receivable, to buy equipment and supplies, to pay current bills, and to repay loans. In addition, an accountant can determine how much cash will come from collection of accounts receivable and how much will have to be borrowed or pulled from an existing line of credit. While working out the cash requirements, your accountant may notice and call your attention to danger spots, such as accounts that are past due.

If you're applying for a loan, your accountant can assemble financial information, for example, a profit-and-loss or income statement and a balance sheet. The purpose of such data is to show the lender the financial position of your business and its ability to repay the loan. Using this information, your accountant can advise you on whether you need a short-term or long-term loan. If you have never borrowed before, your accountant may help you by introducing you to a lender who knows and respects the accountant's reputation. This, alone, may be worth the cost of hiring an accountant.

Taxes are another area in which an accountant can contribute advice and assistance. Normally, a record-keeping system that provides the information you need for making profitable decisions will suffice for tax purposes. However, if you purchase equipment that requires special depreciation, have employees who handle cash or require payroll taxes, or have extensive bad debts, a good accountant can help you identify the problems, suggest a method of keeping good records, and help you minimize your tax obligation by writing off bad debts as a business expense. Accounting firms will also get your federal and state withholding numbers for you, instruct you on where and when to file tax returns, prepare tax returns, and do general tax planning for your small business.

In looking for an accountant, get referrals from trusted friends, business associations, professional associations, and other business services. Discuss fees in advance and draw up a written agreement about how you will work together. Your accountant is your key financial adviser. He or she should alert you to potential danger areas and advise you on how to handle growth spurts, how to best plan for slow business times, and how to financially mature and protect your business future from unnecessary risk.

How to Hire an Insurance Agent

A good insurance agent is as valuable to your success as any other professional consultant. An experienced and trustworthy insurance agent can both reduce your exposure to risk and keep your insurance costs to a minimum.

Ask around among other business services and professionals for recommendations of a good insurance agent. If possible, search for one who primarily serves the business community rather than the family or individuals. They will better know your problems and concerns. Travel services often require errors and omissions insurance as well as standard business insurance.

Ask prospective agents for some advice on a specific problem. Don't tell them what you think the solution is. Their responses can help you determine who are the best at cost-effective problem solving.

The agent is the insurance industry's primary client representative. Typically, the independent agent is a small business owner and manager. By using this distribution system, insurance companies are represented by agents who receive a commission for selling the companies' products and services. An independent agent may represent more than one insurance company.

Liability insurance coverages, particularly for property damage and bodily injury, usually include legal defense at no additional charge when the policyholder is named a party to the lawsuit that involves a claim covered by the policy. Litigation is costly, whether the claimant's suit is valid or frivolous. The legal defense provision greatly reduces these costs to you.

Action Guidelines

Starting up your travel service requires a number of important steps: testing your business idea, estimating start-up costs, selecting your business name, locating your business, choosing the form of your business, and selecting your professional advisors. Here's how to implement what you've learned in Chapter 4.

✔ Start writing your business plan. Refer to *The Business Planning Guide,* by David H. Bangs, Jr., and other resources for worksheets and examples.

✔ Write your business's statement of purpose.

✔ Select your business name and find out how to register and protect it in your state.

✔ Develop a slogan or motto that best fits your business.

✔ Decide where to initially locate your business. Research and consider many locations, writing information in your travel business notebook.

✔ Contact your state employment office and other government offices regarding employment laws and requirements. Also let them know about your services.

✔ Decide which form of business you will initially use: proprietorship, partnership, corporation, or limited liability company.

✔ Find a good attorney.

✔ Find a good accountant.

✔ Find a good insurance agent.

MANAGING YOUR TRAVEL SERVICE DAY-TO-DAY

S tarting a business is only part of your goal. To succeed you must manage its daily operation. You must control operating costs, keep and analyze records, price and produce effective travel services, hire and manage employees, and pay taxes.

This chapter covers these and other responsibilities of your travel service's daily operations as suggested by successful business men and women. It will help you understand and focus on the nuts and bolts of your business as you keep your eyes on the broader purpose of your venture: to help others as you help yourself.

Estimating Operating Costs

Managing your travel service business requires that you manage your business budget so you can continue to provide service, support, and employment to others as well as a profit to yourself. When you first started your business, you established a preliminary budget. Now that your business is operating, you must establish an operating budget.

A budget is a forecast of all cash sources and cash expenditures. It is organized in the same format as a financial statement, and most commonly covers a 12-month period. At the end of the year, the projected income and expenses in the budget are compared to the actual performance as recorded in the financial statement.

A budget can greatly enhance your chances of success by helping you estimate future needs and plan profits, spending, and overall cash flow. A budget allows you to detect problems before they occur and to alter your plans to prevent those problems.

In business, budgets help you determine how much money you have and how you will use it, as well as help you decide whether you have enough money to achieve your financial goals. As part of your business plan, a budget can help convince a loan officer that you know your business and have anticipated its needs.

A budget will indicate the cash required for necessary labor and materials, the day-to-day operating costs, the revenue needed to support business operations, and expected profit. If your budget indicates that you need more revenue than you can earn, you can adjust your plans by:

- reducing expenditures (hiring independent contractors or part-time, rather than full-time, employees, purchasing less expensive furniture, eliminating an extra telephone line),
- expanding sales (offering additional services, conducting an aggressive marketing campaign, hiring an additional reservations agent), and/or
- lowering your salary or profit expectations.

There are three main elements to a budget: sales revenue, total costs, and profit.

Sales are the cornerstone of a budget. It is crucial to estimate anticipated sales as accurately as possible. Base estimates on actual past sales figures. Once you target sales, you can calculate the related expenses necessary to achieve your goals.

Total costs include fixed and variable costs. Estimating costs is complicated because you must identify which costs will change—and by how much—and which costs will remain unchanged as sales increase. You must also consider inflation and rising prices as appropriate.

Variable costs are those that vary directly with sales. Paper and printer toner expenses are examples of variable costs for your travel service business. Fixed costs are those that don't change regardless of sales volume. Rent is considered a fixed cost, as are salaries. Semivariable costs, such as telephone expenses, have both variable and fixed components. Part of the expense is listed as fixed (telephone line charges), and part is variable (long distance charges).

Profit should be large enough to make a return on cash investment and your labor. Your investment is the money you put into the firm at start-up and the profit that you have left in the firm (retained earnings) from prior years. If you can receive 10 percent interest on $10,000 by investing outside of your business, then you should expect a similar return when investing $10,000 in equipment and other assets within the business. In targeting profits, you also want to be sure you're receiving a fair return on your labor. Your weekly paycheck should reflect what you could be earning elsewhere as an employee.

Budgeting Operating Costs

As you develop your budget, you'll be working with the budget equation. The basic budget equation is:

> **Sales = Total Costs + Profit**

This equation shows that every sales dollar you receive is made up partly of a recovery of your costs and partly of profit. Another way to express the basic budgeting equation is:

> **Sales – Total Costs = Profit**

This equation shows that, after reimbursing yourself for the cost of producing your service, the remaining part of the sales dollar is profit. For example, if you expect $1,000 for a specific job and you know that it will cost $900 to market and perform this service, your profit will be $100.

In calculating an operating budget, you will often make estimates based on past sales and cost figures. You will need to adjust these figures to reflect price increases, inflation, and other factors. For example, during the past three years, a travel agent spent an average of $1,500 on advertising costs per year. For the coming year, the owner expects an advertising cost increase of 5 percent (0.05). To calculate next year's advertising costs, the owner multiplies the average annual advertising costs by the percentage price increase ($1,500 X 0.05 = $75) and adds that amount to the original annual cost ($1,500 + $75 = $1,575). A shortcut method is to multiply the original advertising cost by one plus the rate of increase ($1,500 X 1.05 = $1,575).

If your travel service business is a new venture and has no past financial records, rely on your own experience and knowledge of the industry to estimate demand for and costs of your service. Your accountant or trade association may also be able to help you develop realistic estimates.

Before you create an operating budget, you must answer three questions:

- How much net profit should you realistically expect your business to generate during the calendar year?
- How much will it cost to produce that profit?
- How much sales revenue is necessary to support both profit and cost requirements?

To answer these questions, consider expected sales and all costs—either direct or indirect—associated with your travel service. To make the safest estimates when budgeting, most companies prefer to overestimate expenses and underestimate sales revenue.

Start constructing your budget with either a forecast of sales or a forecast of profits. For practical purposes, most small businesses start with a forecast of profits. In other words, decide what profit you realistically want to make and then list the expenses you will incur to make that profit.

Keeping Accurate Records

Why keep records? There are many reasons. For the individual just starting a travel service business, an adequate record-keeping system increases the chances of survival. Also an established travel service can enhance its chances of staying in business and increasing profits with a good record-keeping system.

Keeping accurate and up-to-date business records is, for many people, the most difficult and uninteresting aspect of operating a business. If this area of business management is one that you believe will be hard for you, plan now how you will handle this task. Don't wait until tax time or until you're totally confused. Take a course at a local community college, ask a volunteer SCORE representative, or hire an accountant to advise you on setting up and maintaining your record-keeping system.

Here are some of the questions that good business records can answer:

- How much business am I doing?
- How much credit am I extending?
- How are my collections?
- What are my losses from credit sales?
- Who owes me money?
- Who is delinquent?
- Should I continue extending credit to delinquent accounts?
- How much cash do I have on hand?
- How much cash do I have in the bank?
- Does this amount agree with what records tell me I should have, or is there a shortage?
- How much have I invested in supplies?
- How much do I owe my travel suppliers and other creditors?
- How much gross profit or margin did I earn?
- What were my expenses?
- What's my weekly payroll?
- Do I have adequate payroll records to meet the requirements of workers' compensation insurance, wage-and-hour laws, social security insurance, unemployment compensation insurance, and withholding taxes?
- How much net profit did I earn?
- How much income tax will I owe?
- Are my sales, expenses, profits, and capital showing improvements or did I do better last year than this?
- How do I stand as compared with two periods ago?
- Is my business's position about the same, improving, or deteriorating?
- On what services am I making a profit, breaking even, or losing money?
- Am I taking full advantage of cash discounts for prompt payments?
- How do the financial facts of my travel service business compare with those of similar businesses?

Get the point? Your business requires a good record-keeping system to help you work smarter rather than harder.

Your records will be used to prepare tax returns, make business decisions, and apply for loans. Set aside a special time each day to update your records. It will pay off in the long run with more deductions and fewer headaches. A good record-keeping system should be:

- simple to use,
- easy to understand,
- reliable,
- accurate,
- consistent, and
- timely.

Several published systems and software systems provide simplified records, usually in a single record book. These systems cover the primary records required for all businesses, but some are modified specifically for the travel service business. Check your local office supply store, your trade association, or trade journals for more information on specialized record books.

Simply, your records should tell you these three facts:

1. How much cash you owe

2. How much cash is owed to you

3. How much cash you have on hand

To keep track of everything, you should have these basic journals:

- A sales journal (Figure 5.1, on page 92, shows the business transaction, when and for whom it was performed, and the amount of the sale.
- A cash receipts register (Figure 5.2, on page 93) shows the amount of money received, from whom, and for what.

Sales Journal

ABC Travel Service

PERIOD ENDING:

Date	Check Number	To Whom	For What	Account	Amount

Figure 5.1: Sales journal for travel services

ABC Travel Service

Cash Receipts Register

PERIOD ENDING: May 30 1995

Date	Check Number	Account Number	Amount	Name
May 2 1995	4321	9876	$2,500.00	Mary Jefferson - Hawaii trip
May 7 1995	6543	8765	$1,100.00	Smith & Smith - Las Vegas convention deposit
May 11 1995	2109	6565	$3,200.00	John Williams - Final payment on South American cruise

Figure 5.2: Cash receipts journal for travel services.

- A cash disbursements register (Figure 5.3, on page 95) or check register shows each check disbursed, the date of the disbursement, number of the check, to whom it was made out (payee), the amount of money disbursed, and for what purpose.

- A general journal for noncash transactions and those involving the owner's equity in the business.

In addition, here are other records you will need in your business:

- Accounts Receivable is the record of accounts on which you are due money from a sale for which you haven't been fully paid.

- Accounts Payable is the record of accounts for which you will have to pay money because you have purchased a product or service but haven't paid for it all.

- Equipment is a record of your firm's investment in equipment that you will use in providing your service and will not normally resell.

- Payroll is a record of the wages of employees and their deductions for income, FICA, and other taxes as well as other payroll deductions. Figure 5.4, on page 96, is a typical weekly time report from which payroll information is gathered.

Some businesses combine all of these journals into a single journal. In fact, there are many good one-write systems available that allow you to make a single entry for each transaction. You can also use computer software such as Quicken, Quick-Books, Microsoft Money, or Manage Your Money to track income and expenses in a checkbook format. More extensive accounting software programs include Peachtree Accounting and M.Y.O.B. (Mind Your Own Business).

ABC Travel Service				Cash Disbursements Register	
				PERIOD ENDING: May 30 1995	
Date	Check Number	Account Number	Amount	Name	
May 1 1995	1234	5678	$850.00	Johnson Realty - Lease payment	
May 3 1995	1235	9876	$243.00	AT&T - Telephone bill	
May 5 1995	1236	3210	$790.00	Bradfordd Wholesale Travel Services - Tour deposit	
May 8 1995	1237	7654	$3,000.00	Barbara Simmons - Capital draw	

Figure 5.3: Cash disbursements journal for travel services.

ABC Travel Service

WEEKLY TIME REPORT

LOCATION / ORG. UNIT

DATE

NAME	HOURS	CLASSIFICATION	DESCRIPTION OF WORK
Benjamin Samson	34	Agent	Res agent
Joanne Brown	40	Office Manager	Answered phones, kept books, printed tickets and plans
Helen Noone	20	Outside agent	Sold travel services to own clientele

REMARKS

The undersigned employee certifies that the above and foregoing is the actual, correct number of hours worked by him/her on the day stated, and that he/she has not been told or instructed by anyone having authority over him/her to incorrectly state the number of hours actually worked.

Employee's Signature _____

Supervisor's Signature _____

Figure 5.4: Weekly time report for employees of a travel service.

Single Entry and Double Entry

There are two ways to record transactions in your business: with a single entry or with a double entry. The primary advantage to single-entry record keeping is that it is easy. As the name implies, you make a single entry that records the source of each income or destination of each expense. Each entry is either a plus or a minus to the amount of cash that you have. Receipt of a check on an outstanding account is a plus. Payment of a supplies order is a minus. As long as you have a limited number of transactions, single-entry accounting is adequate.

But as your travel service grows in complexity, you will want a check-and-balance system that ensures that records are accurate. Double-entry accounting requires that you make two offsetting entries that balance each other. A check received on an outstanding account is a debit to Cash and a credit to Accounts Receivable. Payment for a supplies order is a debit to Supplies and a credit to Cash.

Every account has two sides: a left or debit side and a right or credit side. The posted debits must always equal the posted credits. Some types of accounts are called debit accounts because their balance is typically a debit. Asset accounts (Cash, Accounts Receivable) are debit accounts. Liability accounts (Accounts Payable, Notes Payable) usually carry a credit balance. Income carries a credit balance while expenses carry a debit balance. Everything else within double-entry bookkeeping is based on the above rules.

If, at the end of the month, the debits don't equal the credits, check for debits erroneously posted as credits, credits erroneously posted as debits, transposition of numbers (123 to 132), and incorrect math.

Here are some examples of common double entries:

- Cash income = debit Cash and credit Income
- Credit or accrued income = debit Accounts Receivable and credit Income
- Cash expense = debit Expense Account and credit Cash
- Credit or accrued expense = debit Expense Account and credit Accounts Payable
- Prepaid expense = debit Prepaid Expenses and credit Cash.

Assets, Liabilities, and Net Worth

Assets include not only cash, inventory, land, building, equipment, furniture, and the like, but also money due from individuals or other businesses (known as Accounts or Notes Receivable).

Liabilities are funds acquired for a business through loans or the sale of property or services to the business on credit. Creditors do not acquire ownership in your business, but promissory notes to be paid at a designated future date (known as Accounts or Notes Payable).

Net worth (or shareholders' equity or capital) is money put into a business by its owners or left in it as retained earnings for use by the business in acquiring assets.

The formula for this structure is:

Assets = Liabilities + Net Worth

That is, the total funds invested in assets of the business are equal to the funds supplied to the business by its creditors plus the funds supplied to the business by its owners. If a business owes more money to creditors than it possesses in value of assets owned and retained earnings, the net worth or owner's equity of the business will be a negative number.

This accounting formula can also be expressed as:

$$\text{Assets} - \text{Liabilities} = \text{Net Worth}$$

Cash and Accrual

Many small businesses are operated primarily on a *cash basis*. The customer buys products with cash and the merchant buys inventory with cash or short-term credit. As businesses become larger and more complicated, many keep records on the accrual basis. The dividing line between cash basis and accrual basis might depend on whether or not credit is given to customers as well as the amount of inventory required.

Accrual basis is a method of recording income and expenses in which each item is reported as earned or incurred, without regard as to when actual payments are received or made. Charge sales are credited at once to Sales and charged to Accounts Receivable. When the bills are collected, the credit is to Accounts Receivable.

Accruals should also be made for larger expense items payable in the future, such as annual or semi-annual interest on loans.

If you're comfortable with accounting, accrual can be the most accurate basis for records. But the cash basis is easiest to understand. As long as you don't prepay many of your expenses and are not incorporated, a cash basis is fine for your new travel service business.

Managing Accounts Receivable

Income not paid to you is called *Accounts Receivable.* Here are a few rules that can help you keep Accounts Receivable current. First, be sure bills are prepared immediately after the service is performed and the statement is mailed to the correct person and address and contains sufficient information to fully identify the source and purpose of the charge. Note that some businesses will simply set aside any bills that they question.

At the end of each month, age your Accounts Receivable. That is, list accounts and enter the amounts that are current, unpaid for 30 days, and those more than 60 days old. In fact, most Accounts Receivable computer programs will produce reports on aged receivables, then call each account in the 60 plus days column and find out why the bill is unpaid. Keep an especially close watch on larger accounts.

To ensure that you get paid promptly, pay close attention to customers' complaints about bills. If a complaint is justified, offer an adjustment and reach an agreement with the customer. Then get a date from the customer as to when you can expect to receive the payment.

Managing Payroll Records

Quarterly and yearly reports of individual payroll payments must be made to federal and, in many cases, state governments. Each individual employee must receive a W-2 form by January 31 showing total withholding payments made for the employee during the previous year.

A payroll summary should be made each payday showing the employee names, employee numbers, rates of pay, hours worked, overtime hours, total pay, and amount of deductions for FICA (social security insurance), Medicare insurance, state and federal withholding taxes, deductions for insurance, pension, savings, and child support, as required.

To ensure that you maintain adequate records for this task, keep an employee card for each employee of your firm. The employee card or computer file should show the full legal name, social security insurance number, address, telephone number, name of next of kin and their address, marital status, number of exemptions claimed, and current rate of pay. A federal W-4 form completed and signed by the employee should also be attached to the employee card or record.

Also maintain a running total of earnings, pay and deductions for each individual employee.

To begin your payroll system, contact the Internal Revenue Service (Washington, DC 20224) and request the Employer's Tax Guide (Circular E) and get a nine-digit Employer Identification Number. The IRS will then send you deposit slips (Form 8109) with your new ID number printed on them. Use these deposit slips each time you pay your payroll taxes. Payroll taxes are paid within a month of the ending of a quarter; that is, January 31, April 30, July 31, and October 31. As your business grows, you may be required to pay payroll taxes more frequently. By then, your accountant will help you determine your needs and the process.

Managing Petty Cash

Most business expenses will be paid by business check, credit card, or placed on account with the seller. However, there may be some small expenses that will be paid by an employee or with cash that requires reimbursement. Because the amount is typically small, the fund from which the reimbursement comes is usually known as *petty cash*.

A petty cash fund should be set up to be used for payments of small amounts not covered by invoices. A check should be drawn for, say, $100. The check is cashed and the fund placed in a box or drawer. When small cash payments are made for such items as postage, shipping, or supplies, the items are listed on a printed form or even a slip of paper. When the fund is nearly exhausted, the items are summarized and a check drawn to cover the exact amount spent. The check is cashed and the fund replenished. At all times, the cash in the drawer plus the listed expenditures should equal the established amount of the petty cash fund.

Equipment Records

Keep an accurate and up-to-date list of permanent equipment used in your travel service business. Especially, keep track of equipment useful for a year or longer and of appreciable value. Equipment records should show date purchased, name of seller, description of item, check number of payment(s), and amount of purchase including tax. If you own a number of items, keep a separate list for vehicles, computers and printers, and office furniture and fixtures. From these records you will develop a depreciation worksheet and provide supporting information for fixed asset accounts.

A charge to expenses should be made to cover depreciation of fixed assets other than land. Fixed assets are any item you purchase to use in your business for a year or longer. Examples are buildings, vehicles, equipment, furniture, and office fixtures. Smaller businesses will usually charge depreciation at the end of their fiscal year, but if your business grows and you have major fixed assets, you or your accountant may decide to calculate depreciation monthly.

As clarification, a calendar year is 12 consecutive months beginning January 1 and ending December 31. A fiscal year is 12 consecutive months ending on the last day of any month other than December. A short tax year is less than 12 months because your firm was not in business a full year or you have changed your tax year.

How Travel Services Are Priced

A travel service sells a product from a travel provider, for which the service receives a commission. So pricing isn't an issue for travel services as it would be for shoe stores or CD shops. Even so, pricing is important as many travel services offer discounts, rebates, and refunds to customers who use higher levels of travel services. A profitable travel service must understand pricing.

Travel providers—such as airlines, hotels, and car rental agencies— set their prices based on the three Cs of pricing:

- Cost
- Competition
- Customer

For example, a shuttle airline will determine the cost to fly from point A to point B. This cost includes the cost of the aircraft, fuel, flight and ground crews, terminal space, advertising, and many other expenses. They typically break this down into the cost-per-passenger-mile.

The second consideration is the competition. If an airline's cost is $128 for a flight and their competitor is offering it for $120, the airline will probably lower their price below cost in order to retain business. On the other side, if the competition is pricing the ticket at $250, you can bet the airline will price theirs at or about $250.

The third element in the price formula is the customer. If there are insufficient customers, the price may go down to attract new ones. Or it may go up to cover the loss of seats.

How do the three Cs of pricing impact your travel service? You are in a position to be able to shop price based on your knowledge of cost, competition, and customers.

Selling Value

Humorist Robert Benchley said it best: "In America there are two classes of travel: first class, and with children." Actually, you can serve both markets—first class and with children—as long as you sell appropriate value to each market.

How can a fancy restaurant charge five times as much as the diner next door for the exact same ingredients? They sell value. Call it ambiance or image or snobbery or nonprice considerations or whatever. The fancy restaurant makes the client's purchase an event rather than just a transaction. The fancy restaurant treats the client like a person rather than a number, gives extra service, uses finer dinnerware, and decorates the food to look more appetizing.

You'll see the same technique—selling value rather than price—in any competitive business where one firm wants to stand out above the others. Chevys are sold on price; Cadillacs are sold on value—and both are built by General Motors. Value says that, whether the price is large or small, you will get your money's worth.

So how does a travel agent sell value? By offering services that other travel services do not, by paying attention to the details, or by simply turning questions of price into discussions of value.

There are many extra services that a valuable travel agent can perform for clients that don't cost much to implement yet add value to his or her service. Some travel services offer free shuttle service to and from the airport. The cost to the travel service business is minimal and is usually factored into the price, but the extra-mile service is a courtesy that your competitors may not offer.

Value-priced travel service can step ahead of its competition by taking on small, low-commission travel services in order to get its name out to travelers. Once clients come to an agent for his or her service, then the agent can describe the value of purchasing travel upgrades. This service gives the travel agent another chance to sell his or her value to the client or prospect.

Imagine seeing on the grocer's shelf a can of tomato sauce that was discolored and dented, the label torn. You'd probably pass it by for one that looked neat, fresh, and undamaged. Yet the contents of each can may be exactly the same quality. Appearance does make a difference—especially in the travel service business. For just a few dollars more, your business can develop a clean, professional appearance that will tell prospects and customers that you offer quality. Keep your office neat and orderly. Dress professionally. Always wear a smile.

Price is the cost of something. Value is the worth of something. Why is your service worth something?

- You're knowledgeable; you know about travel service and how to perform a valuable service.
- You're efficient; you know how to work smart to get the job done in less time.
- You're honest; you will not knowingly mislead your client or forget to tell them about discount opportunities.
- You're helpful; you want to solve the client's travel problems not just perform a job.
- You're fair; you charge a reasonable fee for an important service.
- You're accessible; you respond to questions, you answer telephone calls, you follow up with clients.

Successful travel services don't shun the question of pricing or apologize for not discounting their services. They look forward to the question so that they can explain why their service is worth more than that of other travel agents. They sell—and deliver—value.

How to Hire Good Employees

The best way to hire the right person for the job is to clearly define what skills are needed. Once you know what it takes to do the job, you can match the applicant's skills and experience to the job's requirements. This step will probably be easy for you if you're hiring a travel agent, but how about office help or other support functions?

Once you have a job description on paper, decide what skills the person must have to fill the job. Then, estimate the value of this service to your business. Finally, determine how much other employers in your area are paying for these skills.

When you know the kinds of skills you need in your new employee and their market value, you're ready to contact sources that can help you recruit job applicants.

Each state has an employment service (Department of Employment, Unemployment Bureau, or Employment Security Agency). All are affiliated with the United States Employment Service, and local offices are ready to help businesses with their hiring problems. The state employment service will screen applicants for you by giving aptitude tests (if any are available for the skills you need). Passing scores indicate the applicant's ability to learn the work, so be as specific as you can about the skills you want.

Private employment agencies will also help in recruitment. However, the employee or the employer must pay a fee to the private agency for its services. This fee can be from a month's to as much as a year's salary.

Another source of applicants is a "Help Wanted" sign in your own office window (if you have one). Of course, a lot of unqualified applicants may inquire about the job, and you cannot simultaneously interview an applicant and talk on the phone to a customer.

Newspaper advertisements are another source of applicants. You reach a large group of job seekers, and if you use a blind box address, you can screen them at your convenience. If you list an office phone number, you may end up on the phone with an applicant instead of with a customer.

Job applicants are readily available from local schools. The local business school may offer courses for those wanting to enter the travel industry. Hire a student on a part-time basis to help during your busy season. Many part-time students continue with their employer after they finish school.

You may also find job applicants by contacting friends, neighbors, customers, suppliers, current employees, local associations, service clubs, or even a nearby armed forces base where people are leaving the service. However, don't overlook the problems of such recruiting. What happens to the goodwill of these sources if they recommend a friend whom you do not hire, or if you have to fire the person they recommend?

Your choice of recruitment method depends on what you're looking for, your location, and your method of managing your business. You have many sources available to you. A combination may serve your best needs. The important thing is to find the right applicant with the correct skills for the job you want to fill, whatever the source.

A good employee is one who is skilled, reliable, and trustworthy. You may be the best judge of the applicant's skills, but how do you test reliability? Fortunately, there are standardized tests you can administer to measure potential of substance abuse, courtesy, maturity, conscientiousness, trustworthiness, commitment, and attitudes toward safety. One such test is produced by Wonderlic Personnel Tests, Inc. (1509 N. Milwaukee Ave., Libertyville, IL 60048; 800-323-3742) and requires about 15 minutes to complete the 81 true/false statements. The test is available in paper and computerized versions and costs less than $12 each. Wonderlic also offers a personnel test that measures the applicant's ability to understand instructions, potential for learning a job quickly, ability to solve job related problems, and ability to work creatively. Such tests can help you profitably find and manage better employees.

Understanding and Paying Taxes

Like it or not, the government is your business partner. And, as your partner, they receive a portion of your profits—even before you do. However, government can also help you make a profit through the Small Business Administration, Department of Commerce, state corporate divisions, and numerous other business services.

The owner-manager of a small business plays two roles in managing taxes. In one role, you're a debtor. In the other, an agent or tax collector, whether you want to be or not.

As a debtor, you're liable for various taxes, and you pay them as part of your business obligations. For example, each year, you owe federal income taxes, which you pay out of the earnings of your business. Other tax debts include state income taxes and real estate taxes.

As an agent, you collect various taxes and pass the funds on to the appropriate government agency. If you have employees, you deduct federal income, social security insurance, or FICA taxes, and, in some states, you collect state income taxes from the wages of your employees. If your state requires sales tax on your travel service business, you will collect it from your customers.

If you are a proprietor, you pay your income tax as any other individual citizen. Your income, expenses, and profit or loss are calculated on Schedule C, which is filed with your annual Form 1040. A partnership files its own tax forms and passes the profits on to the partners for filing on their personal income tax forms. A corporation files on IRS Form 1120 or short form 1120A. Sub-chapter S corporations file on IRS Form 1120S. Self-employment tax—social security insurance for the self-employed—is reported on your IRS 1040 Form using Schedule SE.

Individual proprietors and partners are required by law to put the federal income tax and self-employment tax liability on a pay-as-you-go basis. That is, you file a Declaration of Estimated Tax (Form 1040 ES) on or before April 15, then make payments on April 15, June 15, September 15, and January 15.

Income tax returns from a corporation are due on the 15th of the third month following the end of its taxable year, which may or may not coincide with the calendar year. To find out more about your tax obligations, contact your regional IRS office (or call 1-800-829-3676) for the following publications:

IRS Publications

- *Tax Guide for Small Business* (Publication 334)
- *Guide to Free Tax Services* (Publication 910)
- *Your Federal Income Tax* (Publication 17)
- *Employer's Tax Guide* (Circular E)
- *Taxpayers Starting a Business* (Publication 583)
- *Self-Employment Tax* (Publication 533)
- *Retirement Plans for the Self-Employed* (Publication 560)
- *Tax Withholding and Estimated Tax* (Publication 505)
- *Business Use of Your Home* (Publication 587)

In addition, there are a number of federal forms you'll need for good record keeping and accurate taxation:

- Application for Employer Identification Number (Form SS-4) if you have employees
- Tax Calendars (Publication 509)
- Employer's Annual Unemployment Tax Return (Form 940)
- Employer's Quarterly Federal Tax Return (Form 941)
- Employee's Withholding Allowance Certificate (W-4) for each employee
- Employer's Wage and Tax Statement (W-2) for each employee
- Reconciliation/Transmittal of Income and Tax Statements (W-3)
- Instructions for Forms 1120 and 1120A for corporate taxes

Action Guidelines

As you can see, there are many responsibilities to managing the day-to-day operation of your travel service. They include controlling operating costs, keeping helpful records, offering quality travel services at fair prices, managing employees, and paying required taxes. Here are some things you can do today to apply what you've learned in this important chapter.

✔ Estimate your travel service's operating costs.

✔ Develop an estimated operating budget for your travel service including sales, costs, and profit.

✔ Design or select a simple record-keeping system, including journals and ledgers or accounting software.

✔ If you plan to hire employees, establish a payroll system.

✔ Set up equipment records.

✔ List ways you can sell value over price.

✔ Develop your own process for producing effective travel service.

✔ Establish a simple but usable time-management system.

✔ Call the IRS toll-free number to order appropriate booklets and forms.

Chapter

6

MARKETING YOUR
TRAVEL SERVICE

"Never a ship sails out of bay but carries my heart as a stowaway," says Roselle Montgomery. The allure of travel is great. Travel sells itself.

What is your travel service's market?

A market is simply the group of prospects who would most benefit from certain services. The market for your travel service is made up of those who potentially could benefit from your service—a very broad definition that will apply to you and to your competitors. Defining *your* travel service's market means determining the characteristics of those who would most benefit from your unique combination of knowledge, skills, and resources.

This chapter will help you define your market and help you efficiently reach it.

Understanding Marketing

The first step to defining your market is to define who you are to them. Because there are dozens of types of travel agents—

and hundreds of potential markets—we will use broad examples. But you'll quickly get the idea and be able to apply it to your specialty.

For example, how would you define the market for a travel business of one person who can only work evenings and weekends but cannot use the home for an office? A prospect for this service is someone who is currently working and cannot take time off work to come to an office. In fact, not having a regular office can be turned into a marketing advantage of meeting in the convenience of their home for the interview. Take notes on a laptop computer, then do the actual work at home, a public library, or other site. By defining these unique benefits, a travel service can best define its prospects or market.

Let's say that the best opportunity for using your skills is to specialize in travel service for senior citizens. In this example, who are your prospects? Your prospects are those who are retired or semi-retired and want to spend time traveling. So how do you find prospects? First, you go where they go. Depending on your age, you join local seniors' clubs. If you're younger, you find organizations where seniors are primary members.

Here's another example of how successful travel services market. One service owner decided that there were already too many travel agents selling to individuals, so she decided to market exclusively to manufacturers within a large industrial park. She specialized in arranging travel for salespeople. To market her service, she established a database or paper file about every manufacturer's sales manager in her area. She then developed a one-page newsletter with tips on travel services and mailed it to each of her prospects. She could have also faxed copies to make the newsletter seem more timely.

Obviously, how you approach your prospects as a travel agent will be somewhat different. Yet the principles will be the same. You will first determine whether there is sufficient opportunity for you to build your business and whether potential competitors are already adequately serving this market. Then you will focus your attention and your marketing on those who can best use your services.

Who are your prospects? They are those who have been influenced by your advertising as well as those recommended to you by satisfied customers. They are former customers, newcomers to the area, customers who need immediate help, and your competitors' dissatisfied customers. They are people who rarely require travel service as well as those who travel frequently.

Some start-up travel services begin their businesses by serving customers who cannot be served by their current or former employer. By working with them, you reduce the amount of marketing you must do to develop customers. Most start-up travel services then pay a marketing fee or a finders fee to these sources. It's another reason to maintain a good relationship with all of your past and current employers.

Let's look more closely at specifics on how to develop a profitable market for your travel service.

Marketing Your Services

Marketing is a science. It's not a perfect science where the answer to a question is always the same. It's a science based on data, information, knowledge, and wisdom. Data is easy to get and build into information. From this information comes knowledge and, eventually, wisdom. Wisdom is what makes your business profitable. Marketing builds your business.

The purpose of marketing is to get more customers. That's it. If you're new to business, the purpose is to get your first customers. If you've established a substantial business, the purpose is to keep those customers that you have.

There are dozens of ways that you can market your services to prospects and customers. They include the many forms of advertising, as well as literature, direct mail, and telephone marketing.

Identifying Your Customers

Customers are vital to your business. That's obvious. The better quality of customers, the greater the success of your business.

There are two ways of defining prospective customers or prospects: demographics and psychographics.

Demographics is a study of statistics about people: where they live, how much they make, how they buy, what their hobbies are. Retailers use census information to build demographics that help them in deciding where to build a store. Travel services can use demographics, too. They can learn who would use their services and, then, where to find them.

As an example, a travel agent specializing in travel services for college students must know more than the fact that a prospect attends a specific college. The travel agent must also know when a student typically begins planning for travel (spring break, holiday break, the end of the semester), what travel modes students typically use (plane, train, bus, rental car), what students typically pay for such services and who pays (student, parent). This and additional information is available from a number of sources including surveys of the students themselves.

Psychographics is the study of why people buy. You would think that most people buy for logical reasons. However, even in the business world, people often buy for emotional reasons and justify their decision with logical reasons. Knowing why your clients buy will help you sell to them more effectively.

If you've built a solid reputation in your area as a travel agent whose name means quality, you can sell that name. People want to go with a winner, so you will get some travel bookings just because people know you were involved. So learn what makes your customers buy and help them to buy from you.

Understanding your customers is so important that large corporations spend millions of dollars annually on market research. Although some formal research is important, a small business can usually avoid this expense. Typically, the owner or manager of a small travel service knows the prospective customers personally. From this foundation, understanding your customers can be built by systematic effort.

Understanding buyers starts with the realization that they purchase benefits rather than products or services. Consumers don't select travel. They want to be somewhere else. Some want safety. Others look for speed or convenience. Other travelers look primarily for new experiences. A few look only at price.

You must find out, from their point of view, what customers are buying—and why. Understanding your customers enables you to profit by providing what buyers seek: satisfaction.

Finding Prospects for Your Travel Service

A *prospect* is a prospective customer, someone who could potentially use your service but hasn't done so yet. They may not have heard of your service, or they may not know enough about your service to determine its value, or they simply haven't been asked.

Who is a prospect for your travel service? Of course, that depends on what service you perform for customers. If you're a travel agent who specializes in cruises to Hawaii, your prospects are those who have been on or want to be on a cruise ship. To turn these prospects into customers you must first think like they think, only faster. As an example, if a cruise representative tells you that most cruises are taken by couples between 50 and 70 years of age with annual incomes of $35,000 or more, you target that group for your message. You purchase a mailing list of people in this category within your area and send them information about your services. Your chances of selling cruise tickets to them are much greater than selling to the general public.

The U.S. Census Bureau is an excellent source of statistical data for market surveys. Based on the latest decade's census, the bureau divides large cities into census tracts of about 5,000 residents within Standard Metropolitan Statistical Areas (SMSAs). Data on these tracts cover income, housing, and related information that can be valuable to you. Results of the 1990 census are now available. For this and other market information, contact the Office of Business Liaison, U.S. Department of Commerce, Washington, DC 20230. The Bureau of the Census offers business statistics, data, and special demographic studies among its services.

How should you keep track of your prospects? There are many ways, depending on how many prospects there are and how you plan to market to them. Some travel service business owners use 3 x 5 inch index cards available at any stationery store. A typical prospect card will include both basic information—name, owner, address, telephone number, business, etc.—as well as qualifying information and notes from prospective contacts.

If you're using a computer to automate your business records, there are contact management software programs that will help you keep track of prospects. They range in price from about $50 for a simple system to $500 or more for a specialized prospecting system that can even help you write personalized sales letters. As an example, a good contact management program will give you standard fields or areas where you can type the firm name, contact name(s), address, telephone and fax numbers, the names of mutual friends or associations, information about travel preferences (when, how, why), and so on. If you're making regular telephone calls to prospects, the program may help you schedule call-backs, maintain records of conversations, and help you write personalized letters that can be quickly printed for mailing or even faxed to your prospect while they're still thinking about you.

How to Sell Travel Services

The majority of your prospects will make first contact with you by telephone. They may have read your ad in the newspaper or phone book, or heard about you from a mutual acquaintance. In any case, it is vital that you make the most of this first contact, answering their questions while getting answers to your own questions about them.

The prospect wants to know:

- Why should I use your service?
- Are you qualified to help me with my travel needs?
- Are your services of greater value than the price?
- Are you trustworthy?

You want to know:

- What's your name and how can I contact you?
- How did you hear about my service?
- What do you need to know to make a decision to book your travel through me?

How to Upgrade Travel Services

An honest travel service will not try to sell a client something they cannot afford. But only the client can tell you what they can afford. Most clients aren't sure exactly what travel will cost. They want value for their travel dollar. Your job as a travel service is to describe the benefits and value of travel to those who are deciding if they can afford the cost.

For example, you've quoted a price for a business trip to Cincinnati. "You can enjoy the extra comfort, service, and

quality food as a first class passenger for an additional $82."
It's then the client's decision whether the value is worth the price.

Whether you specialize in destination or mode travel, or sell general travel services, make the customer aware of the value and cost of available ugrades. Never push them.

Cost-Effective Advertising

The purpose of advertising is to tell your potential customers how they will benefit from using your services. The best way to do so is to let your other customers tell your prospects about their success with your service. That's called word-of-mouth advertising and it's the most valuable type of advertising there is. Unfortunately, it is also the slowest to develop. Your first satisfied client may, in conversations, mention your good service once or twice a month. After hearing that a number of times and if they are looking for your service, a prospect may call you for your service. By that time you may be out of business due to lack of work.

Travel services must advertise. How much should you spend on advertising? Successful travel services typically spend about 8 percent of their estimated commission income on advertising. This can be as low as 5 percent or as high as 10 percent. For example, a travel service with estimated annual net income of $100,000 should spend between $5,000 and $10,000 a year on advertising and promotion. Services located in areas where competition is tough may spend more. Remember, advertising percentages are based on net income (commissions) rather than gross income (travel service sales).

Fortunately, many travel providers offer cooperative, or co-op, advertising. That is, they will pay part of your advertising costs if their product is prominently promoted in the ad. Ask your travel providers or suppliers how to qualify for co-op advertising money.

Successful travel service owners suggest that the majority of an advertising budget should be spent during months when business is typically slower. Rather than an ad budget of $250 a month, slow months may require a budget of $400 or more, while busy months will have a budget of $100. Long-term advertising, such as the phone book's Yellow Pages, requires monthly payments.

Advertising is based on impressions. Every time that your prospect sees or hears your name, you make what's called an impression. It may be something small like seeing the sign in front of your business or an ad in the local paper. Or it may be a listing in the Yellow Pages or a positive (or negative) comment made by a mutual acquaintance.

Each impression is cumulative. After numerous impressions, large and small, your prospect may bring your name into the possible source part of his or her brain. Then, when a legitimate need for your service arises, the prospect considers you as a supplier. Think about it. How many times did you see or hear about Honda or Mr. Coffee before you even considered trying their product. Probably dozens or even hundreds of impressions were made. And consider that any negative feelings about these products are also impressions.

The point is that you will need to positively impress your prospects many times and in many ways before they can be upgraded to a customer.

Besides advertising, there are numerous ways you can make positive impressions on prospects. One successful travel agent developed and presented a no-charge Saturday seminar on traveling by train. Those who came were obviously excellent prospects for her services as a train travel agent.

In addition, travel agents can speak to other groups on a variety of travel topics. Kiwanis, Rotary, Lions, and other service organizations are always looking for informative—and free—speakers. Just remember that it must be informative, not just an opportunity to sell.

Make sure you have an effective brochure that you can give to people who want to know more about your service.

Many successful travel services develop much of their business through referrals. That is, they sell their services to those who work with people looking for jobs: counselors, human resources departments, businesses, employment offices, and executive placement centers.

Of course, you can enhance word-of-mouth advertising by developing testimonials. That is, when you have a client who expresses satisfaction with your service, you ask the client to write you a testimonial letter. The letter, on business stationery, will describe how professional your service is and how well you respond to the needs of customers.

Unfortunately, only a small percentage of those who say they will write a testimonial letter will actually do so. But the problem isn't sincerity, it's time. Most customers just don't have the time to write such a letter. So some travel services offer to write a draft of the letter themselves and send it to the customer for approval and typing on their letterhead. A well-written testimonial from a well-respected person can be worth thousands of dollars in new business to you. You will copy it and include it in with your brochure, quote from it in advertisements, and pass it out to prospects. It will be your best form of advertising.

Of course, make sure that you have a customer's written permission to use any testimonials you quote in advertising.

Free Publicity

There are many effective ways that you can advertise your travel service at little or no cost. Exactly which methods you use depends somewhat on your specialization.

Once you have your business card printed, carry a stack of them with you wherever you go. Pass them out to anyone who may be or know a prospect. As you stop for lunch, put your business card on the restaurant's bulletin board. Do the same if you stop at a local market for anything: put your card on their bulletin board. All it costs is the price of a business card. In fact, order separate business cards for your specialties, such as travel services for adventure-seekers, regional travel tours, and convention bookings.

Many travel services overlook one of the best sources of free advertising—publicity. As you start your business, write a short article or press release, and give copies to your local newspaper, radio stations, shoppers, and other media. Include in it information about your business, such as names of owners, experience, affiliations, background, expertise, purpose of the business, location, target market, and contact name. If your market is across an industry rather than a geographic area, send this press release to magazines in that particular trade, called trade journals.

You can promote your business and get free advertising by offering to write a weekly newspaper column on travel in exchange for an ad in the paper. The weekly column cannot be self-serving, but the ad certainly can.

If you're personable and would be comfortable doing so, offer to host a radio call-in talk show on travel or a related topic. Or you can become a regular guest on someone else's talk show. The publicity will make you a local celebrity as well as an authority on travel.

Cable TV also offers opportunities for travel service owners who want to creatively market themselves. Talk with your local cable operator about current and upcoming channels that may need your services.

Also consider establishing an award or scholarship at a local high school, trade school, or community college in your business's name. Not only will you be able to deduct the award as a legitimate business expense, you can also use the award to promote your business in the local media.

One more proven idea—seek awards. Join professional and business associations, entering all applicable business contests. If you win any of them, from first place to honorable mention, use the award as an opportunity to promote your business through local and national media.

Newspaper Advertising

The majority of homes in the U.S. and Canada receive a daily or weekly newspaper or a shopper. From the advertiser's point of view, newspaper advertising can be convenient because production changes, if necessary, can be made quickly. Also, you can often insert a new advertisement on short notice, depending on the frequency of the publication. Another advantage is the large variety of ad sizes that newspaper advertising offers. The disadvantages to newspaper advertising include the cost of a large ad, which is required to stand out among other large ads; the short-life throwaway nature of a newspaper; and the poor printing quality of newspapers. If you do decide to advertise in newspapers, establish a consistent schedule rather than a hit-and-miss advertising program. Most important, ensure that the program is realistically within your budget.

Most travel services advertise in the travel section of their local newspaper. Depending on the size of the community, the frequency of the paper, and the cost, an ad in the business or leisure sections can be a valuable investment. Find out where your competitors are advertising and develop a better ad. You may want to use a name like ABC Travel Service to ensure that your ad is listed first, or prominently include a feature or benefit that your competitors don't offer.

If there is sufficient savings, sign a contract for a specific number of column inches of advertising each year rather than a standard size. By doing so you are earning a discount as well as allowing for business fluctuations. Reduce the size of your ad when business is good and increase it when you need more business. Some contracts will allow you to change your ad as much as once a week while still earning a substantial discount.

Yellow Pages Advertising

Many travel services say that an ad in the Yellow Pages is one of their best sources of new business. In most locations, if you purchase a required business telephone line, you will get a listing in one category of your local telephone book. In some areas, this is optional. The listing may be as simple as:

```
ABC Travel Service, 123 Main St......555-1234
```

Or the firm name can be in capital letters such as:

```
ABC TRAVEL SERVICE
123 Main St.................................555-1234
```

Or you can include information on your specialty, and even an alternate telephone number like this:

```
ABC Travel Service
Specializing in Business Travel
123 Main St.................................555-1234
If no answer..............................555-2345
```

Many businesses upgrade their listings with space ads. A space ad is simply an advertisement that takes up more space than a line or two and is usually surrounded by a box.

To determine the size and cost of an appropriate space ad, check your local and nearby telephone book's Yellow Pages under headings for "Travel Agencies & Bureaus." Look for ads from competitors. When a potential client looks in their Yellow Pages, which ads stand out best? Which have the greatest eye-appeal? Which are easiest to read? Remember that you don't need the largest ad in the phone book; you need the one that's most cost-effective for you.

The last few pages in your Yellow Pages frequently have information on how to select a space ad. You'll see terminology like double half, double quarter, triple quarter, and columns. It's actually quite easy to follow. Most larger telephone books have four vertical columns per page; community phone books in rural areas are half-size with only two columns per page. So a triple quarter is three columns wide and a quarter page long; a double half is two columns wide and a half page long.

At the end of the Yellow Pages, there will often be a toll-free telephone number for ordering a space ad or listing. Or you may find the number in the front of the phone book under Business Telephone Service or a similar title. Also ask about cost and availability of color in your ad. The firm that produces your telephone book will help you design and write your ad. Then they will supply a layout of the ad and a contract for you to sign. Most Yellow Pages listing or space ad contracts are for one year and can be paid in monthly installments.

Building Repeat Business

A repeat customer is simply one who uses your services more than once. If the customer is satisfied and needs travel services again, you have a good chance of getting a repeat customer. You didn't have to go out and spend additional money on advertising or work extra hours to promote your business. Your quality of business promotes itself.

The best way to get repeat business is to ask for it. As you call up your clients to determine their satisfaction, also ask them:

- Do you have any other planned trips coming up?
- Would you like us to help you plan them?
- What travel services do you expect to need in the coming year?

- Are there any travel questions you have that I can answer?

You can also build repeat business by continually trying to sell your services to them. It is more productive to get more business from current customers than to find new ones. Here's how some successful travel services build repeat business:

- Write a monthly newsletter to all customers with new information on travel opportunites as well as a listing of the services you offer.
- Perform value-added services, like delivering tickets to the customer's home or place of business.

Earning Referral Business

Earning referrals is one of the most powerful types of business promotion. A referral is simply having one of your satisfied customers sell your services to prospective buyers. The word of a trusted businessperson is much more believable to prospects than is the word of an unknown businessperson or salesperson.

So how do you get your customers to refer prospects to you? You ask them to do so. In fact, it should be an automatic question that you ask: Is there anyone you know who may also be traveling soon? Ask it right after you book travel, as you interview a client, and—especially—whenever anyone compliments an aspect of your work.

"I really appreciate the tour of the Holy Land that you booked for us. We enjoyed it so much."

"I'm glad to hear that. Is there anyone whom you know who may also want to visit the Holy Land soon?"

In addition, once your customer has referred others to you, many feel a stronger obligation to continue to use your services. It will not only help you grow your business, but will also help you keep the customers that you have.

Action Guidelines

Learning how to effectively market your travel service can quickly separate you from your competition. There have been many proven marketing ideas offered in this chapter. To implement some of these ideas for your travel business, take the following actions:

✔ Define your travel service's market. Who are your prospects? Who needs and will buy travel services from you?

✔ Start a database of prospective customers or referral sources.

✔ How and why do your prospective customers buy travel services? What are their expectations?

✔ Learn what your prospects have in common with each other. Do they read a specific newspaper or are they members of a certain group?

✔ Establish a low-cost advertising campaign for reaching your prospective customers. Ask travel providers about co-op advertising opportunities.

✔ Find customers who will write testimonial letters for you or allow you to write them on their behalf.

✔ Carry a stack of your business cards wherever you go and post them wherever you can.

✔ Develop a cost-effective Yellow Pages ad with the help of your telephone company's advertising department.

✔ Establish your own techniques for developing repeat and referral business as suggested in this chapter.

MANAGING YOUR TRAVEL SERVICE'S MONEY

M oney certainly isn't *everything*. But it is a convenient way of keeping score. In most cases, you will be monetarily rewarded in relation to the service you provide to others. The more you help the more you earn. How much of that you keep depends on how well you manage your money.

The purpose of this chapter is to ensure that you gain and keep an appropriate amount of money for what you do. It covers profits, cash flow, credit, financing, and other money topics.

Tracking Profit and Loss

Profit is simply the amount of money you have left over once you've paid all of your expenses. If you have more expenses than income, you have a loss. Pretty simple.

Of course, there's much more to profit and loss than numbers on paper. Your business can actually show a profit on paper, yet not have any cash. In fact, many profitable businesses go out of business each year because of negative cash flow.

How can you keep the cash flowing in your travel service business? By keeping good records, watching expenses, and tracking the flow of cash in and out of your business. Before we cover cash flow, let's see how successful travel services set up and use an efficient money-tracking system.

Tracking Your Money

As the owner of a travel service business, you need accurate information on a regular basis to ensure that your business is running smoothly. As a single-person firm, you may have all the information you need in your head. But as your firm grows, you will need some information daily, other information weekly, and still other data on a monthly basis. Let's take a look at what you will need and when.

In order to manage your travel service firm, you will want the following information on a daily basis:

- Cash on hand
- Bank balance
- Daily summary of sales and cash receipts
- Daily summary of monies paid out by cash or check
- Correction of any errors from previous reports

You can either prepare this information yourself, have an office employee prepare it for you, or rely on your accountant. While daily records will not show trends, they will help you get a feel for the level of business that you're doing. And you'll be able to spot problems before they become serious.

Once a week, you or someone in your employ should prepare a weekly report on your firm. While still not sufficient for long-term planning, weekly figures will help you make small corrections in the course your business is taking. Weekly, you'll want the following reports:

- Accounts Receivable Report listing accounts that require a call because they are more than 60 days past due
- Accounts Payable Report listing what your business owes, to whom, and if a discount is offered for early payment
- Payroll Report including information on each employee, the number of hours worked during the week, rate of pay, total wages, deductions, net pay, and related information
- Taxes and reports required to be sent to city, state, and federal governments

Your weekly reports should be prepared by the end of business each Friday so you can review them over the weekend or early Monday morning.

Once a month, you should review a number of pieces of information that have accumulated through your daily and weekly reports but were too small to analyze clearly. Now that they are part of a full month, information about cash flow, Accounts Receivable, and other parts of your business make more sense—and can be more easily acted upon. Here are some of the reports and information you will want to see every month:

- Monthly summary of daily cash receipts and deposits
- General ledger including all journal entries
- Income statement showing income for the prior month, expenses incurred in obtaining the income, overhead, and the profit or loss received
- Balance sheet showing the assets, liabilities, and capital or current worth of the business

- Check reconciliation showing which checks were deposited and which were applied by payees against your business checking account, and verifying that the cash balance is accurate
- Petty cash fund report to ensure that paid-out slips plus cash equals the beginning petty cash balance
- Tax payment report showing that all federal tax deposits, withheld income, and FICA, state, and other taxes have been paid
- Aged Receivables Report showing the age and balance of each account (30, 60, 90 days past due)
- Summary of Schedule C entries

Let's cover three of the most important documents you'll review monthly: your income statement, your balance sheet, and your cash flow forecast.

Your Income Statement

An income statement (Figure 7.1, on page 135) is a tally of the income from sales and the expenses incurred to generate the sales. It is a good assessment tool because it shows the effect of your decisions on profits. It is a good planning tool because you can estimate the impact of decisions on profit before you make them.

Your income statement includes four kinds of information:

1. Sales information lists the total revenues generated by the sale of your service to clients.

2. Direct Expenses include the cost of labor and materials to perform your service.

3. Indirect Expenses are your costs even if your service is not sold, including salaries, rent, utilities, insurance,

Income Statement

ABC Travel Service

June, 1995

INCOME

Commissions

Airlines	6,157
Tour services	3,211
Wholesalers	4,732
Misc. income	1,213
Total Income	**15,313**

EXPENSES

Owner's Salary	3,500
Payroll	4,750
Rent	1,200
Office Equipment and Supplies	1,480
Telephone and Utilities	445
Insurance	752
Dues and miscellaneous	610
Total Expenses	**12,737**

NET PROFIT (before income taxes)	**2,576**

Figure 7.1: Simplified income statement.

depreciation, office supplies, taxes, and professional fees.

4. Profit is shown as pre-tax income (important to the IRS) and after-tax or net income (important to you and your loan officer).

Your Balance Sheet

A balance sheet (Figure 7.2, on page 136) is a summary of the status of your business—its assets, liabilities, and net worth—at an instant in time. By reviewing your balance sheet along with your income statement and your cash flow forecast, you will be able to make informed financial and business planning decisions.

```
                        Balance Sheet
                        ABC Travel Service

ASSETS
Current Assets
   Cash                                              26,321
   Accounts Receivable                                5,120
      less allowance for doubtful accounts             256
   Prepaid Expenses                                   2,191
Total Current Assets                                 33,376
Fixed Assets
   Computer system                                    8,275
   Land                                              47,000
   Building                                          82,500
Total Fixed Assets                                  137,775
TOTAL ASSETS                                        171,151

LIABILITIES AND EQUITY
Current Liabilities
   Accounts Payable                                   4,332
   Real estate mortgage                              94,300
   Owner's Equity                                    72,519
TOTAL LIABILITIES AND EQUITY                        171,151
```

Figure 7.2: Simplified balance sheet.

The balance sheet is drawn up using the totals from individual accounts kept in your general ledger. It shows what you have left when you pay all your creditors. Remember: *Assets less Liabilities equals Capital or Net Worth.* The assets and liabilities sections must balance—hence the name. It can be produced quarterly, semiannually, or at the end of each calendar or fiscal year. If your record keeping is manual you will be less likely to develop a frequently updated balance sheet. Many accounting software programs can give you a current balance sheet in just a couple of minutes.

While your accountant will be most helpful in drawing up your balance sheet, it is you who must understand it. Current Assets are anything of value you own such as cash, inventory, or property that the business owner can convert into cash within a year. Fixed Assets are things such as land and equipment. Liabilities are debts the business must pay. They may be current, such as amounts owed to suppliers or your accountant, or they may be long-term, such as a note owed to the bank. Capital, also called Equity or Net Worth, is the excess of your assets and retained earnings over the amount of your liabilities.

Your Cash Flow Forecast

Your business must have a healthy flow of working capital to survive. Cash flow is the amount of working capital available in your business at any given time. To keep tabs on cash flow, forecast the funds you expect to disburse and receive over a specific time. Then you can predict deficiencies or surplus in cash and decide how best to respond.

A cash flow forecast (Figure 7.3, on page 138) serves one other very useful purpose in addition to planning. As the actual information becomes available to you, compare it to the monthly cash flow estimates you previously made to see how accurately you are estimating. As you do this, you will be giving your self on-the-spot business training in making more accurate estimates and plans for the coming months. As your ability to estimate improves, your financial control of the business will increase.

Every time that you have to purchase on credit, you add interest costs to your business. If you had more cash you would be able to save more on interest expense. For this and other reasons, you can reduce your costs by increasing cash flow.

The cash flow forecast identifies when cash is expected to be received and when it must be spent to pay bills and debts. It shows how much cash will be needed to pay expenses and when it will be needed. The cash flow forecast enables you to plan for shortfalls in cash resources so short-term working cap-

ABC Travel Service

Cash Flow Forecast

DATE: Apr 1 1995
FOR TIME PERIOD: Second Quarter
APPROVED BY:
PREPARED BY:

FOR INTERNAL USE ONLY

	Date: Apr 30 1995		Date: May 30 1995		Date: Jun 30 1995	
	ESTIMATE	ACTUAL	ESTIMATE	ACTUAL	ESTIMATE	ACTUAL
Opening Balance	11,234.00	10,934.00	11,531.00	11,731.00	12,225.00	12,334.00
Collections From Trade	5,280.00	4,921.00	5,667.00	5,822.00	5,950.00	5,123.00
Misc. Cash Receipts	1,258.00	1,715.00	1,520.00	1,433.00	1,620.00	1,559.00
TOTAL CASH AVAILABLE	$17,772.00	$17,570.00	$18,718.00	$18,986.00	$19,795.00	$19,016.00
DISBURSEMENTS						
Payroll	1,945.00	1,955.00	1,945.00	1,936.00	1,945.00	1,989.00
Trade Payables	2,111.00	1,945.00	2,200.00	2,111.00	2,300.00	1,980.00
Other	786.00	765.00	822.00	754.00	833.00	875.00
Capital Expenses	789.00	899.00	800.00	812.00	820.00	844.00
Income Tax	2,123.00	2,192.00	2,123.00	2,146.00	2,123.00	2,111.00
Bank Loan Payment	567.00	567.00	567.00	567.00	567.00	567.00
TOTAL DISBURSEMENTS	$8,321.00	$8,323.00	$8,457.00	$8,326.00	$8,588.00	$8,366.00
Ending Balance	$9,451.00	$9,247.00	$10,261.00	$10,660.00	$11,207.00	$10,650.00
Less Minimum Balance	$10,000.00	$10,000.00	$10,000.00	$10,000.00	$10,000.00	$10,000.00
CASH AVAILABLE	($549.00)	($753.00)	$261.00	$660.00	$1,207.00	$650.00

Figure 7.3: Simplified cash flow forecast.

ital loans—or a line of credit—may be arranged in advance. Also, if you have excess cash, it allows you to put this cash to productive use and earn a return. It allows you to schedule purchases and payments so you can borrow as little as possible. Because not all sales are cash sales, you must be able to forecast when Accounts Receivable will be cash in the bank as well as when regular and seasonal expenses must be paid.

The cash flow forecast may also be used as a budget, helping you increase your control of the business through comparing actual receipts and payments against forecasted amounts. This comparison helps you identify areas where you can manage your finances even better.

A cash flow forecast or budget can be prepared for any period of time. However, a one-year budget matching the fiscal year of your business is the most useful. Many successful travel services prepare their cash flow forecasts on a monthly basis for the next year. It should be revised no less than quarterly to reflect actual performance in the previous three months of operations and verify projections.

All businesses, no matter how small or large, function on cash. Many businesses become insolvent because they don't have enough cash to meet their short-term obligations. Bills must be paid in cash, not potential profits. Sufficient cash is, therefore, one of the keys to maintaining a successful business.

Travel services face a continual cycle of events that may increase or decrease the cash balance. Cash is decreased in the acquisition of tickets, equipment, or supplies. It is reduced in paying off the amounts owed to travel suppliers (Accounts Payable). Travel services are sold and these sales generate money owed from customers (Accounts Receivable). When customers pay their travel bill, Accounts Receivable is reduced and the Cash Account is increased. However, the cash flows are not necessarily related to the sales in that period because customers may pay in the next period.

Travel services must continually be alert to changes in working capital accounts, the cause of these changes, and their implications for the financial health of the company. The change in the cash can be readily determined if you know net working capital and the changes in current liabilities and current assets other than cash.

Let:

NWC = net working capital
CA = change in current assets other than cash
CL = change in current liabilities
Cash = change in cash

Net Working Capital is the difference between the change in current assets and current liabilities:

$$NWC = CA + Cash - CL$$
$$Cash = NWC - CA + CL$$

This relationship shows that if we know the net working capital (NWC), the change in current liabilities (CL), and the change in current assets less cash (CA - cash), we can calculate the change in cash. The change in cash is then added to the beginning balance of cash to determine the ending balance.

At any given level of sales, it's easier to forecast the required Accounts Payable and Receivables than net working capital. To forecast this net working capital account, you must trace the sources and application of funds. Sources of funds increase working capital. Applications of funds decrease working capital. The difference between the sources and applications of funds is the net working capital.

The following calculation is based on the fact that the balance sheet is indeed in balance. That is, the total assets equal total liabilities plus owner's equity.

Current Assets + Noncurrent Assets + Retained Earnings = Current Liabilities + Long-term Liabilities + Equity

Rearranging this equation:

Current Assets – Current Liabilities = Long-term Liabilities + Equity – Noncurrent Assets – Retained

Because the left side of the equation is working capital, the right side must also equal working capital. A change in either side affects the net working capital. If long-term liabilities and equity increase or noncurrent assets decrease, net working capital increases. This change would be a source of funds. If noncurrent assets increase or long-term liabilities and equity decrease, net working capital decreases. This change would be an application of funds.

Typical sources of funds or net working capital are funds provided by operations, disposal of fixed assets, issuance of stock, and borrowing from a long-term source. The typical applications of funds or net working capital are purchase of fixed assets, payment of dividends, retirement of long-term liabilities, and repurchase of equity.

How to Improve Cash Flow

As you can see, to grow your travel service business you need cash. Once you've analyzed cash flow and determined that you need more of it, what can you do? Depending on the specific type of business you own, you can find increased cash in your Accounts Receivable and in your inventory.

Accounts Receivable represent the extension of credit to support sales. In your business, the types and terms of credit you grant are set by established competitive practices. As an investment, the Accounts Receivable should contribute to overall Return on Investment (ROI).

Excessive investment in Accounts Receivable can hurt ROI by tying up funds unnecessarily. One good way to judge the extent of Accounts Receivable is to compare your average collection period with that of rivals or the industry average. If your average collection period is much higher than your competitors' or the industry norm, your Accounts Receivable may be excessive.

If they are excessive, it may be that you're not keeping tight control of late payers. You can check this by developing an aging schedule. An aging schedule shows the distribution of Accounts Receivable with respect to being on time or late.

Failure to closely monitor late payments ties up investment and weakens profits. The more overdue accounts become, the greater is the danger that they will be uncollectable and will have to be written off against profits.

If the aging schedule does not reveal excessive late accounts, your average collection period may be out of line simply because your credit policy is more liberal than most. If so, it should translate into more competitive sales and greater profits. Otherwise, you should rethink your credit program.

Developing Your Business's Credit

Credit is simply someone's faith that a customer will keep a promise. You buy a computer system on credit, and the lender believes that you will pay back what you've borrowed—or, in the case of secured loans, you have assets that can be sold to cover what you've borrowed.

A good way to start building your business credit is to use personal assets—signature, real estate equity—as collateral for your business. One enterprising travel service owner simply applied for a credit card in his business name from the same company that sponsored his long-standing personal credit card. He asked for a small credit limit, used it and paid it off, then asked for an increased credit limit. Meantime, he used the credit card as a reference for a new account with a supplier. Other beginning business people have used equity in their homes or investment land as collateral for credit with banks and suppliers.

Travel services that sell airline tickets are required to post a $20,000 bond or irrevocable letter of credit with the ARC to ensure that they will pay for the tickets they buy.

Where and How to Get a Loan

A recent survey of small businesses reported that 23 percent had lines of credit, 7 percent had financial leases, 14 percent had mortgage loans, 12 percent had equipment loans, and 25 percent had vehicle loans. For larger firms, the percentages about double in each category.

The ability to get a loan when you need it is as necessary to the operation of your business as is the right equipment. Before a bank or any other lending agency will lend you money, the loan officer must feel satisfied with the answers to these five questions:

1. What sort of person are you, the prospective borrower? In most cases, the character of the borrower comes first. Next is your ability to manage your business.

2. What are you going to do with the money? The answer to this question will determine the type of loan and its duration.

3. When and how do you plan to pay it back? Your lender's judgment of your business ability and the type

of loan will be a deciding factor in the answer to this question.

4. Is the cushion in the loan large enough? In other words, does the amount requested make suitable allowance for unexpected developments? The lender decides this question on the basis of your financial statement, which sets forth the condition of your business, and on the collateral pledged.

5. What's the outlook for business in general and for your business in particular?

When you set out to borrow money for your firm, it is important to know the kind of money you need from a bank or other lending institution. Let's discuss loans and other types of credit. There are numerous types of loans available, all with their own unique name depending on the lender.

Signature Loan. A signature loan holds nothing in collateral except your promise to pay the lender back on terms with which you both agree. If your monetary needs are small, you only need the loan for a short time, your credit rating is excellent, and you're willing to pay a premium interest rate because you're not using physical collateral, a signature or character loan is an easy way to borrow money in a hurry.

Credit Cards. Many a small business has found at least some of its funding in the owner's personal credit card. Computers, printers, books, office supplies, office overhead, and other costs can be covered with your personal credit card. However, interest rates on credit cards are extremely high—sometimes double of what you might pay on a collateral loan. But credit cards can offer you quick cash when you need it. If this is an option for you, talk to your credit card representative about raising your credit limit. It will be much easier to do so while you're employed by someone else.

Line of Credit. A line of credit is similar to a loan except that you don't borrow it all at once. You get a credit limit, say $50,000, that you can tap anytime you need money for business purposes. The most common is the revolving line of credit that you can draw from when business is off and pay back when business is good, providing that you don't exceed your limit. A line of credit is an excellent way for a travel service to work through the ups and downs of seasonal business. With some restrictions, a line of credit can be established using a portion of your home equity as collateral. Using a secured equity earns you a lower interest rate.

Cosigner Loan. A cosigner loan should be one of the most popular loans for small businesses, but many business people never consider it. Simply, you find a cosigner or a comaker with good credit or assets who will guarantee the loan with you. If you have a potential investor who believes in your business but doesn't want to put up the cash you need, ask him or her to cosign for a loan with you. Your chances of receiving the loan are much better. Some cosigners will require that you pay them a fee of 1 to 4 percent of the balance or a flat fee; others will do it out of friendship or the hope of future business from you. In any case, consider this as an excellent source of capital for your new travel service.

Equipment Leases. If you're purchasing equipment, computers, or other assets for your business, the supplier may loan or lease the equipment to you. This often requires about 25 percent down so be ready to come up with some cash of your own.

Collateral Loan. A collateral loan is one in which some type of asset is put up as collateral; if you don't make payments you will lose the asset. So the lender wants to make sure that the value of the asset exceeds that of the loan, and will usually lend 50 to 75 percent of asset value. A new travel service owner often does not have sufficient collateral—real estate or equipment—to secure a collateral loan unless an owner uses personal assets such as a home.

Passbook Loan. Sometimes you can get a loan by assigning a savings account to the bank. In such cases, the bank gets an assignment from you and keeps your passbook. If you assign an account in another bank as collateral, the lending bank asks the other bank to mark its records to show that the account is held as collateral.

Life Insurance Loan. Another kind of collateral is life insurance. Banks will lend up to the cash value of a life insurance policy. You have to assign the policy to the bank. If the policy is on the life of an executive of a small corporation, corporate resolutions must be made authorizing the assignment. Most insurance companies allow you to sign the policy back to the original beneficiary when the assignment to the bank ends. Some people like to use life insurance as collateral rather than borrow directly from insurance companies. One reason is that a bank loan is often more convenient to obtain and may often be obtained at a lower interest rate.

For more information on business credit, write to the Federal Trade Commission, Washington, DC 20580; Attn: Public Reference. Ask for their booklet *Getting Business Credit.* It's free.

Managing Interest Rates

Money is a commodity, bought and sold by lenders. Just like other products, you can often save money by shopping around. Here are some points to consider as you shop for money.

First, are there any loan fees or other charges required to set up or service the loan? Some lenders will require that a loan fee of 1 or 2 percent, or more, be paid in advance. Others will even roll the loan fee into the loan—so you actually pay interest upon interest. Others will deduct a monthly service fee from each payment as it is made. This arrangement is not necessarily bad; after all, the lender must make his profit from you in some manner. Just make sure that you understand what the actual cost of the loan is before you agree to it. You also need to know actual interest rates as you compare rates between lenders.

Second, consider whether your best option is fixed rate or variable rate interest. Fixed rate interest means that the interest rate charged by the lender is the same throughout the life of the loan. Variable rate interest can vary during the term of the loan based on some outside factor. This factor is usually the cost of the money to the lender. Most variable interest loans have caps, specifying a maximum amount the rate can rise, both annually and through the life of the loan. The difference between the lender's cost and what he charges you is called the spread. From that spread comes his sales costs, office overhead, salaries, and profit. The spread is also based on the amount of risk he is taking in loaning the money to you. Higher risk means a higher spread. There are numerous indexes used to establish the cost of money. Review all of the options with your lender, ask which one makes the most sense for your needs, and get a second opinion.

Keep in mind that variable rate interest reduces the amount of risk the lender is taking, especially on long-term loans. He is virtually assured that, unless the money market goes crazy and goes over the cap, he will get his margin of profit from every dollar you send him. Lower risk means lower rates. The point is that you shouldn't disqualify variable rate loans from consideration. In many cases, they cost less than fixed rate loans and many lenders are more willing to make them.

To make sure that you pay the best interest rate available, don't jump into the arms of the first loan offer that comes to you. Shop around and compare. You may eventually decide to take that first offer, but only because you've found nothing better.

But don't worry about getting the absolute lowest interest rate available. You may want to accept your regular lender's loan terms, even though it's a quarter of a percentage point higher, in order to maintain a mutually profitable relationship. That quarter point may only mean a few dollars to you and will reinforce your business relationship with your lender.

SBA Guaranteed Loans

Erskine Bowles, SBA administrator, is making sweeping changes to the Small Business Administration, increasing funds and reducing paperwork. As an associate administrator recently announced, "What we're trying to do is get capital into the hands of people who have been capital starved." This is good news for your travel service.

The volume of business loans guaranteed by the SBA has increased from $3 billion in 1989 to approximately $9 billion in 1995. According to the SBA, the average loan was for $250,626 over a term of 11.5 years. About one-fifth of these loans went to companies that were less than two years old. Also important is that paperwork requirements for SBA guaranteed loans has been cut from as many as 40 pages to just 6 pages for loans over $100,000 and a single page for loans under that amount. Here is a summary of current SBA loan opportunities:

SBA 7(a) Guaranteed Loans. Private lenders make SBA 7(a) Guaranteed Loans, which can be guaranteed up to 80 percent by the SBA. Most SBA loans are made under this guaranty program. The maximum guaranty of loans exceeding $155,000 is 85 percent. SBA has no minimum size loan amount and can guarantee up to $750,000 of a private sector loan. SBA provides special inducements to lenders providing guaranteed loans of $50,000 or less. The lender must be a financial institution who participates with the SBA. The small business submits a loan application to the lender. After the initial review, if the lender cannot provide the loan directly, it may request an SBA guaranty. The lender then forwards the application and its analysis to the local SBA office. If approved by the SBA, the loan is closed with the lender, which disburses the funds.

SBA Direct Loans. SBA Direct Loans of up to $150,000 are available only to applicants unable to secure an SBA-guaranteed loan. Direct loan funds are available only to certain types of borrowers, such as handicapped individuals, nonprofit sheltered workshops for disabled workers, Vietnam-era veterans, disabled veterans, businesses in high-unemployment areas and owned by low-income individuals, or for businesses located in low-income neighborhoods. The applicant must first seek financing from at least two banks in their area.

SBA Microloans. The newest SBA loan opportunity, microloans, is intended for smaller businesses who want to get started or grow and only need a few thousand dollars. There is $65 million in microloan money available to small businesses. The typical SBA microloan is for about $10,000, though the limit is $25,000 for worthwhile small business ventures. Contact your regional SBA office for additional information and requirements.

Loan Applications. If you're interested in applying for an SBA guaranteed or direct loan, call your regional office of the Small Business Administration. Even better, ask for the name of an SBA-certified lender in your area. The SBA loan program, notorious for its paperwork requirements, can be expedited by a lender that knows how to work within the system. You'll get your loan faster. In fact, those bankers that have preferred-lender status can handle your SBA loan without the SBA even being involved.

Offering Credit to Customers

Most successful travel services are strict about a no-credit policy. Some require all fees up front with the travel order. Most travel services are paid by credit card. Those that offer credit require that the customer complete a credit application, available at most stationery stores.

Using credit card services, such as Visa, MasterCard, American Express, and Discover, can transfer bad debt problems to others and increase cash flow for your business. However, there is an initial setup cost and ongoing service charges. The credit card service will charge you a service charge of between 2 and 5 percent on each transaction. Talk with your lender or the Airlines Reporting Corporation (ARC) about offering your customers the option of paying for services with their credit card.

Improving Financial Planning

Financial planning affects how and on what terms you will be able to attract the funding you need to establish, maintain, and expand your business. Financial planning determines the human and physical resources you will be able to acquire to operate your business. It will be a major factor in whether or not you will be able to make your hard work profitable.

The balance sheet and the income statement are essential to your business, but they are only the starting point for successful financial management. The next step is called ratio analysis. Ratio analysis enables you to spot trends in a business and to compare its performance and condition with the average performance of similar businesses in the same industry. To do this, compare your ratios with the average of other travel services as well as with your own ratios over several years. Ratio analysis can be the most important early warning indicator for solving business problems while they are still manageable.

One note before we get into ratios: members of trade associations often will share their balance sheet, income statement, and management ratios with other members through studies and reports published by the association. It's just one more good reason to join one of the local or national travel trade associations. These percentages can help you in determining whether your travel service business is being operated as efficiently as other firms in your industry.

Important balance sheet ratios measure liquidity (a business's ability to pay its bills as they come due) and leverage (measuring the business's dependency on creditors for funding).

Liquidity ratios indicate the ease of turning assets into cash. They include the current ratio, quick ratio, and working capital.

Current Ratio. The current ratio is one of the best known measurements of financial strength. It is calculated as follows:

$$\text{Current Ratio} = \frac{\text{Total Current Assets}}{\text{Total Current Liabilities}}$$

The main question this ratio answers is: Does your business have enough current assets to meet the payment schedule of its current debts with a margin of safety? A generally acceptable current ratio is 2:1. That is, twice as many current assets as current liabilities.

Let's say that you—or your lender—decide that your current ratio is too low. What can you do about it?

- Pay some debts.
- Combine some of your short-term debts into a long-term debt.
- Convert fixed assets into current assets.
- Leave in earnings or put profits back into the business.
- Increase your current assets with new equity (bring more cash into the business).

Quick Ratio. The quick ratio is sometimes called the acid test ratio and is one of the best measurements of liquidity. It is calculated as follows:

$$\text{Quick Ratio} = \frac{\text{Cash} + \text{Securities} + \text{Receivables}}{\text{Total Current Liabilities}}$$

The quick ratio is a much more exacting measure than the current ratio. By excluding inventories (typically small in travel service businesses), it concentrates on the really liquid assets with value that is fairly certain. It helps answer the question: If all sales revenues should disappear, could my business meet its current obligations with the readily convertible quick funds in hand?

Working Capital. Working capital is more a measure of cash flow than a ratio. The result of the following calculation must be a positive number:

$$\text{Working Capital} = \text{Total Current Assets} - \text{Total Current Liabilities}$$

Lenders look at net working capital over time to determine a company's ability to weather financial crises. Bank loans are often tied to minimum working capital requirements.

A general rule about these three liquidity ratios is that the higher they are the better, especially if your business is relying heavily on creditor money or financed assets.

Leverage Ratio. The leverage or debt/worth ratio indicates the business's reliance on debt financing (loans) rather than owner's equity. Here's how to figure it:

$$\text{Leverage Ratio} = \frac{\text{Total Liabilities}}{\text{Net Worth}}$$

Net Profit Margin Ratio. Net profit margin ratio is a percentage of sales dollars left after subtracting the cost of goods sold and all expenses, except income taxes. It provides a good opportunity to compare your company's return on sales with the performance of other companies in the industry. It is calculated before income tax because tax rates and tax liabilities vary from company to company for a variety of reasons. The net profit margin ratio is calculated as follows:

$$\text{Net Profit Margin Ratio} = \frac{\text{Net Profit Before Tax}}{\text{Net Sales}}$$

Action Guidelines

Money is the root of all . . . . *business!* It's not that business people are necessarily greedy. They just want some assurance that they will have enough money to continue their business—and their eating habits. Here are some proven ways you can make money and your travel service long-term friends:

✔ Establish a simple system for keeping informed on the financial status of your business on a regular basis.

✔ Watch your balance sheet carefully and learn to apply ratios to ensure success.

✔ Keep a running cash flow forecast, no matter how simple, to ensure that money will continue to come in when you need it.

✔ Learn how to develop and use your net working capital rather than borrow from the bank.

✔ Keep your relationship with your banker open and friendly just in case.

✔ Talk to your banker about becoming a credit card merchant.

BUILDING YOUR TRAVEL SERVICE

T his final chapter offers a collection of ideas and techniques from successful travel service owners and other business people on how to make your business grow. It tells you how to solve small problems before they become big ones, manage employees and temporary help, insure against potential losses for your business and your employees, manage risks and catastrophies, and keep an eye on the future. It will also show you how to better enjoy what you do.

Solving Common Travel Service Business Problems

As the owner of your own travel service business, you deal with problems on a daily basis. So learning how to effectively solve problems can dramatically affect the growth and success of your business. Most business owners solve problems by intuition. By learning the necessary skills, you will become more comfortable with solving problems and reduce the inherent stress of your job.

What is a problem? A problem is a situation that presents an obstacle to your desire to move ahead. Here are a few examples:

- A client just called from Brazil—though they thought they were going to Boise.
- A consortium you frequently use just declared bankruptcy and stranded six of your customers in the Antarctic.
- A computer program doesn't function as it should.
- A part you need for your copy machine is unavailable.
- An employee is undermining your authority with clients.
- New business income is down.
- A customer is complaining about errors in a travel service.
- You're two payments behind on a lease, and they've threatened to repossess your computer.

Where do problems come from? Problems arise from every facet of human and mechanical functions as well as from nature. Some problems we cause ourselves (hiring an untrainable employee). Other problems are caused by forces beyond our control, such as a tornado. Problems are a natural, everyday occurrence of life. However, if mismanaged, they cause tension and frustration that only compounds the problem. Successful business people must learn how to deal with problems in a logical, rational fashion.

Steps to Solving Any Problem

The solutions to some problems, such as how to plan an extraordinarily heavy work load next week, are typically simple and will require only a few moments of contemplation and planning. However, some problems, such as how to increase net income by $100,000 in the next six months, are more critical to your operation and will require more time and effort. In fact, for critical problems, you may want to set aside a full day for analyzing the problem and finding the best solutions.

Recognize the Problem. Before a problem can be solved, you must first recognize that it exists. Here is where your approach to problem solving is crucial. You should not allow the problem to intimidate you. Don't take it personally. Approach it rationally and remind yourself that every problem is solvable if it is tackled appropriately.

Fear of failure can block your ability to think clearly. You can overcome this natural fear if you:

- follow a workable procedure for finding solutions,
- accept the fact that you can't foresee everything,
- assume that the solution you select is your best option at the time, and
- accept the possibility that things may change and your solution fail.

Define the Problem. Once you recognize that a problem exists, your next step is to identify or define the problem itself. You can do so by asking yourself such questions as:

- What exactly happened?
- What started the problem?
- Did something occur that wasn't supposed to?
- Did something break that was supposed to operate?
- Were there unexpected results?

Determine Type. Then ask questions that help you identify the nature of the problem:

- Is this a person, equipment, operational problem?
- What product or service does it involve?

- Is the problem tangible or intangible?
- Is the problem internal or external to the firm?

Evaluate Significance. How important is this problem to the scheme of things? Ask yourself:

- Is this problem disrupting operations?
- Is this problem hampering sales?
- Is this problem causing conflict among people?
- Is this problem affecting personnel and their productivity?
- Is this problem affecting business goals and, if so, which ones?
- Is this problem affecting customers, suppliers, independent contractors, or any other external people?

Estimate Frequency. Some problems are 100-year floods that don't occur often enough to warrant extensive attention. Ask these questions:

- Is it a problem that occurred in the past and the main concern is to make certain that it doesn't occur again?
- Is it a problem that currently exists and the main concern is to clear up the situation?
- Is it a problem that might occur in the future, and the basic concern is planning and taking action before the problem arises?

The answers to these questions will help you focus on the true problem. You can't effectively research the causes of a problem until you have a clear definition of what the problem is. Sometimes, managers spend many hours on what they perceive as the problem only to learn, after seeking the causes, that something else was really the problem.

Selecting the Best Solution

As you answer these questions, you can begin developing a list of possible solutions. Go through this list and cross out those that obviously won't work. These ideas aren't wasted because they affect those ideas that remain. In other words, the best ideas you select may be revised using ideas that won't work.

Break the remaining solution down into its positive effects and negative effects. To do this, some travel service business owners write each solution they are considering on a separate piece of paper. Below the solution, they draw a vertical line down the center of the sheet, labeling one column "Advantages" and the other column "Disadvantages." Finally, they analyze each facet of the solution and its effect on the problem, listing each of the advantages and disadvantages they can think of.

One way to help you think of the advantages and disadvantages is to role-play each solution. Call in a few of your employees and play out each solution. Ask them for their reactions. Based on what you observe and on their feedback, you will have a better idea of the advantages and disadvantages of each solution you're considering.

After you complete this process for each primary solution, select those solutions that have the most significant advantages. At this point, you should be considering only two or three. In order to select the most appropriate solution from these, consider:

- Cost-effectiveness
- Time constraints
- Availability of manpower and materials
- Your own intuition

Before you actually implement the chosen solution, you should evaluate it further. Ask yourself:

- Are the objectives of the solution sound, clear, and simple?
- Will the solution achieve the objectives?
- What are the possibilities that it will fail and in what way?
- How can I reduce the possibility of failure?

Taking Action

Finding the solution doesn't mean that the problem is solved. Now you need to design a plan of action so that the solution gets carried out properly. Designing and implementing the plan of action is equally as important as finding the solution. The best solution can fail because it isn't well implemented.

When designing the plan of action, consider:

- Who will be involved in the solution?
- How will they participate?
- Who will be affected by the solution?
- How will they be affected?
- What course of action will be taken?
- How should this course of action be presented to employees, customers, suppliers, and others?
- When will the action start and be completed?
- Where will this action happen?
- How will this action happen?
- What's needed to make it happen?

Design a plan of action chart including all the details you need to consider to implement the plan and when each phase should happen. Keep in mind, though, that the best plans have setbacks for any number of reasons. A key person may be out for illness or a supplier may ship materials late or a change at the customer's site may require that the timetable be changed.

As each phase of your plan of action is implemented, you should ask yourself whether your goals were achieved, how well they were achieved, and did it work smoothly. To check your own perceptions of the results, get as much feedback as possible from your managers and employees. What you may think is working may not be perceived the same way by those closer to the action. Always remember that customers and employees are your most valuable resources in successfully carrying out your solution.

Managing Employees for Growth

The majority of employees in the labor force are under a merit increase pay system, though most of their pay increases result from other factors. This approach involves periodic review and appraisal of employees' performance.

An effective employee appraisal plan improves two-way communications between the manager and the employee, relates pay to work performance and results, and helps employees understand job responsibilities and expectations and areas for improvement. An employee appraisal plan also provides a standardized approach to evaluating job performance.

Such a performance review helps not only the employee, but also the manager, who can gain insight into the organization. An open exchange between employee and manager can show the manager where improvements in equipment, procedures, or other factors might improve employee performance. Try to foster a climate in which employees can discuss progress and problems informally at any time throughout the year.

To get the best results, use a standardized written form for appraisals. An appraisal form should cover the results achieved, quality of performance, volume of work, effectiveness in working with others in the firm and with customers and suppliers, initiative, job knowledge, and dependability.

To keep your pay administration plan in tune with the times, you should review it at least annually. Make adjustments where necessary and don't forget to retrain supervisory personnel. This isn't the kind of plan that can be set up and then forgotten.

During your annual review, ask yourself if the plan is working for you. That's the most important question. Are you getting the kind of employees you want or are you just making do? What's the employee turnover rate? Do employees seem to care about the business? Most importantly, does your pay administration plan help you achieve the objectives of your business?

Employee Benefits

Employee benefits play an important role in the lives of employees and their families, and they have a significant financial impact on your business. Travel services cannot be competitive employers if they don't develop a comprehensive benefit program. However, if not managed, an employee benefit program can quickly eat up a small firm's profits.

A comprehensive employee-benefits program can be broken down into four components: legally required benefits, health and welfare benefits, retirement benefits, and perquisites.

Legally required benefit plans are mandated by law and the systems necessary to administer such plans are well established. These plans include social security insurance (FICA), workers' compensation insurance, and unemployment compensation insurance (FUTA).

Health and welfare benefits and retirement benefits can be viewed as benefits provided to work in conjunction with statutory benefits to enhance employees' financial security. Health and welfare plans are perhaps the most visible of all the benefit program components. They include medical care, dental care, vision care, short-term disability, long-term disability, life insurance, accidental death and dismemberment insurance, dependent care, and legal assistance.

Retirement plans are established to help ensure that employees are able to maintain their accustomed standard of living upon retirement. Retirement-benefit plans basically fall into two categories: *defined contribution plans*, which provide employees with an account balance at retirement, and *defined benefit plans*, which provide employees with a projected amount of income at retirement.

Perquisite benefits, or perks, are any other benefits an employer promises, such as a company automobile or truck, professional association or club membership, paid tuition, sabbatical, extra vacation, expense account, credit cards, or financial counseling services.

Health and Welfare Plans

When purchasing a health and welfare plan, select an insurance professional whose clientele is made up primarily of small businesses. In fact, if you can find one in your area, select one that's used and recommended by other travel agents. Your insurer needs to be aware of the special problems that face small businesses, especially in your trade. Generous plans that look attractive and logical today may become a financial burden for your growing company. Remember that it is much easier to add benefits than it is to take them away.

Medical plans are usually the greatest concern of employers and employees. There are essentially two kinds of traditional medical plans. Major medical plans cover 100 percent of hospital and inpatient surgical expense as well as a percentage (typically 80 percent) of all other covered expenses. Comprehensive medical plans cover a percentage (again, generally 80 percent) of all medical expenses.

In both types of plans, the employee is usually required to pay part of the premium, particularly for dependents, as well as a deductible. Deductibles often range from $100 to $200 for single coverage and from $200 to $1,000 per person for family coverage.

A comprehensive medical plan is typically less expensive because more of the cost is shifted to the employee. Any plan you design should include features for containing costs.

As an alternative to a traditional medical plan, an employer may contract with a Health Maintenance Organization (HMO) to provide employees with medical services. The main difference between a traditional medical plan and an HMO is that the traditional plan allows employees to choose their medical providers while HMOs often provide medical services at specified clinics or through preferred doctors and hospitals. HMOs trade this flexibility for lower costs that are often passed on to the employee through reduced or eliminated deductibles or lower rates.

Disability insurance is an important but often overlooked benefit in small businesses. Disability insurance prevents a drain of financial resources to support a principal in the event that he or she cannot continue working.

Group life insurance is a benefit employees have come to expect in many regions and trades. Such insurance is usually a multiple of an employee's salary. Be aware that an amount of insurance over a legally specified amount is subject to taxation as income to the employee.

Recent legislation provides that employers who maintain medical and dental plans must provide certain employees the opportunity to continue coverage if they otherwise become ineligible through employment termination or other causes. In addition, new rules state that if a firm's health and welfare plan discriminates in favor of key employees, the benefits to those employees are taxable as income. Talk to your plan administrator about current laws and requirements.

Retirement Benefit Plans

Retirement benefit plans are either *qualified* or *unqualified* plans. A plan is qualified if it has met certain standards mandated by law. It is beneficial to maintain a qualified retirement plan because contributions are currently deductible, benefits earned are not considered taxable income until received, and certain distributions are eligible for special tax treatment.

Of the various qualified plans, profit-sharing plans, 401(k) plans, and defined benefit plans are the most popular.

Profit-Sharing Plans. A profit-sharing plan is a defined contribution plan in which the sponsoring employer has agreed to contribute a discretionary or set amount to the plan. Any contributions made to the plan are generally prorated to each participant's plan account based on compensation. The sponsoring employer makes no promise as to the dollar amount a participant will receive at retirement. The focus in a profit-sharing plan, and in defined contribution plans, is on the contribution. What a participant receives at retirement is a direct function of the contributions. At retirement, profit-sharing plan participants receive an amount equal to the balance in their account. Profit-sharing plans are favored by employers because they allow employers the ability to retain discretion in determining the amount of the contribution made to the plan.

401(k) Plans. Another type of defined contribution plan is the 401(k). In a 401(k) plan, participants agree to defer a portion of their pretax salary as a contribution to the plan. In addition, the sponsoring employer may decide to match all or a portion of the participant deferrals. The employer may even decide to make a profit-sharing contribution to the plan. As described earlier, the focus is on the contribution to the plan. At retirement, participants will receive an amount equal to their account balance. Special nondiscrimination tests apply to 401(k) plans that may reduce the amount of deferrals highly compensated employees are allowed to make, somewhat complicating plan administration. The 401(k) plans are popular because they allow employees the ability to save for retirement with pretax dollars, and they can be designed to be relatively inexpensive.

Defined Benefit Plans. In direct contrast to a defined contribution plan, a defined benefit plan promises participants a benefit specified by a formula in the plan. The focus of a defined-benefit plan is the retirement benefit provided instead of the contribution made. Plan sponsors must contribute to the actuarially determined amounts necessary to meet the dollar amounts promised to participants. Generally, benefits begin at retirement and are paid over the remainder of the employee's life, so a defined benefit plan guarantees a certain flow of income at retirement.

As a business owner, you can establish your own retirement plan, called a Self-Employed Pension (SEP) plan. Call the IRS for a booklet (*Self-Employment Pension Plans*, publication 560) on how to start and manage these plans.

Selecting the Right Plan

Designing and implementing an employee-benefit program can be a complicated process. Many small businesses contract with employee benefit consulting firms, insurance companies, specialized attorneys, or accounting firms to assist in this task. As you establish your program yourself or with a professional, ask yourself:

- What should the program accomplish in the long run?
- What's the maximum amount you can afford to spend on a program?

- Are you capable and knowledgeable in administering the program?
- What kind of program will best fit the needs of your employees?
- Should you involve your employees in the design and selection of the benefit program? If so, how much and at what stage?

Certain plans are more suitable for travel services, based on the employer's financial situation and the demographics of the employee group. Employers who are not confident of their future income may not want to start a defined benefit plan that will require a specific level of contributions. However, if the employees are fairly young, a profit-sharing plan or 401(k) plan can result in a more significant and more appreciated benefit than a defined benefit plan. The 401(k) plans are very popular now that IRAs have been virtually eliminated. However, the nondiscrimination tests make it more difficult for small businesses to maintain 401(k) plans. If your work force is composed mainly of older employees, a defined benefit plan will be more beneficial to them but more expensive for you to maintain.

Remember that while a qualified plan has many positive aspects, the qualified retirement plan area is complicated and well monitored by the government. Make sure you have adequate counsel before you decide on the most appropriate plan for your business.

Hiring Temporary Help

How does your travel service business cope with unexpected personnel shortages? Many businesses are facing this question whether the cause is seasonal peaking, several employees on sick leave, or an unexpected increase in business. For some skills, many travel services hire and use independent contractors or outside agents. But for office work, a growing number hire help through temporary personnel services. In fact, many new travel services will start up their business renting part-time temporary office personnel instead of hiring full-time employees.

Using a Temporary Personnel Service

A temporary personnel service, listed in your phone book's Yellow Pages under "Employment Contractors–Temporary Help," is not an employment agency. Like many service firms, it hires people as its own employees and assigns them to companies requesting assistance. This means that when you use a service, you're not hiring an employee; you're buying the use of their time. The temporary personnel firm is responsible for payroll, bookkeeping, tax deductions, workers' compensation insurance, fringe benefits, and all other similar costs connected with the employee. You're relieved of the burden of recruiting, interviewing, screening, and basic skill training.

Most national temporary personnel companies also offer performance guarantees and fidelity bonding at no added cost to their clients. As important, you're relieved of the need for government forms and for reporting withholding tax, social security insurance, and unemployment compensation insurance.

If you need temporary personnel for a period of six months or more, it's usually more cost-effective to hire a full time employee. Also, if the task requires skills or training beyond basic office skills, it may cost you less to pay overtime to an employee with those skills.

Using Temporary Employees Efficiently

The key to successful use of temporary employees is in planning what type of help you will need, how much, and when.

The accurate information you give to the temporary service firm will improve their efficiency in supplying the correct person for your needs.

Before your temporary employee arrives on the job, there are a few things you should do. First, appoint one of your permanent employees to supervise the temporary employee and check on the progress of the work. Be sure this supervisor understands the job and its responsibilities. Next, let your permanent staff know that you're taking on extra help and that it will be temporary. Explain why the extra help is needed and ask them to cooperate with the new employee in any way possible.

Have everything ready before the temporary employee arrives. The work to be done should be organized and laid out so that the employee can begin producing with a minimum of time spent in adjusting to the job and the surroundings. Also, don't set up schedules that are impossible to complete within the time you allot. Try to stay within the time limits you gave the temporary help service but plan to extend the time period if necessary, rather than hurry the employee.

Finally, furnish detailed instructions. Describe your type of business and the services you offer. Help the temp feel comfortable and part of your team. Most temporary employees have broad business experience and can easily adapt to your requirements—if they know what they are.

Using Independent Contractors

An independent contractor is a self-employed person who performs a service for you. Because an independent contractor is not an employee, you cannot dictate the hours in which the service is performed nor, in many cases, where it will be performed. The advantage of an independent contractor is that they are not on your payroll. They are independent businesspeople who contract their services to you.

Independent travel agents (also known as outside agents) are not salaried employees. They typically don't work in your office. They are contracted to book travel for their clients through your agency. An outside agent will use your ARC and other memberships for settlement. They typically receive a sliding scale of 25 to 50 percent of the total commission.

Many small travel services rely extensively on outside agents to help them during busy times. Some services make it a policy to contract with outside agents rather than hire new employees.

Managing Business Risks

You've learned how to increase sales and reduce expenses for your travel service business. But even as your business grows and profits, you can still lose money. How?

- An employee is injured on the job and sues you.
- An employee runs off with money stolen from your business.
- A fire or flood wipes out your office, equipment, and important records.
- A partner in your business files bankruptcy and the courts attach your business.
- The local economy goes sour and you can't find enough travel business for six months or more.
- A business partner is involved in a divorce settlement and business assets must be sold to meet a court order.
- The IRS comes after you for a large tax bill they think you owe them and takes over your bank account until everything is resolved.

The list goes on. There are many ways that an otherwise profitable business can quickly be thrown into a situation where the business's future is in jeopardy. What can you do about it? First, you can make sure you understand the risks involved in your business. And, second, you can take precautions to ensure that the risks are minimal. They will never go away, but, through smart risk management, you can minimize them and prepare for the worst.

Identifying Potential Risks

Of course, the best time to minimize the risk of business disasters is before they happen. And the first step to minimizing risk is identifying the risks that can occur. Business risks that travel services typically face are:

- Acts of nature (fire, flood)
- Acts of man (theft, vandalism, vehicle accidents)
- Personal injury (employee or user)
- Legal problems (liens, unfair trade practices, torts)
- Financial (loss of income, funding, or assets)
- Taxation (judgments, tax liens)
- Management (loss of owner's capacity to manage or partner's ownership)

Of course, every method of reducing risk—attorneys, insurance, binding agreements, security systems, fire alarms—costs money. So when is it more cost-effective to accept the risk rather than pay for products or services that eliminate the risk? It's a simple question with a simple answer—it all depends.

Actually, the best time to minimize risk in your business is right now. The real answer lies in balancing the cost of loss against the cost of security. There are a number of ways that you can keep your losses to a minimum. They include preventing or limiting exposure to loss, risk retention, transferring risk, and insurance.

One principle of loss prevention and control is the same in business as it is in your personal life: avoid activities that are too hazardous. For example, don't leave cash or valuable equipment where it can be easily stolen.

A travel service business owner may decide that the firm can afford to absorb some losses, either because the frequency and probability of loss are low or because the dollar value of loss is manageable. Maybe your travel service business owns an older vehicle and their drivers have excellent safety records, so you decide to drop the collision insurance on these vehicles but retain it on newer vehicles.

Insuring Against Risks

The most common method of transferring risk is purchasing insurance. By insuring your business and equipment, you have transferred much of the risk of loss to the insurance company. You pay a relatively small amount in premium rather than run the risk of not protecting yourself against the possibility of a much larger financial loss.

Of course, you can be overinsured or pay more than is necessary for the amount of risk that you transfer. That's why it's so important to select a reputable and professional insurance agent to advise you. But in business insurance, only you can decide which exposures you absolutely must insure against. Some decisions, however, are already made for you: those required by law and those required by others as a part of doing business with them. Workers' compensation insurance is an example of insurance that is required by law. Your bank probably won't lend you money for equipment, real estate, or other assets unless you insure them against loss.

Today, very few businesses—and especially travel service— have sufficient financial reserves to protect themselves against the hundreds of property and liability exposures that they face. What those exposures are, what their dollar value is, and how much is enough, are difficult questions. As you build a team of business professionals to help you effectively manage your business, you should use an insurance professional.

Four kinds of insurance are essential to your business: fire, liability, automobile, and workers' compensation insurance. Selecting from among the dozens of available policies and options can be somewhat confusing to most business people. However, the insurance information on pages 174–175 will guide you in making the right decisions for the right reasons.

Managing Business Cycles

No businesses are truly recession-proof. All business have cycles where sales become easier or harder to make. Travel services are subject to the same business cycle that most businesses face. Even so, there are steps you can take to minimize the market's downswing and extend its upswing.

First, determine the business cycle for your market. Reviewing income and financial records from prior years, or checking with the local chamber of commerce, you can draw a chart illustrating the local business cycle. In your region, it may be that most of the market for your service occurs in the spring and summer. Or maybe in the winter and fall. Or the cycle may be fairly equal across the year, but alternate years may fluctuate up or down. The first step to coping with recessions in the local business cycle is to determine exactly what and when that cycle is.

The next step is to begin planning for it. That is, if you're coming up to a typically slower period, determine what you need to do. In past years, how much has income dropped? For how long? Can you find income sources in other specialities where the cycle is moving up? What expenses can you cut? Do you have an employee who would like a seasonal layoff so he can catch up on other interests? Maybe you need to dramatically cut back on your expenses and debts for this period. If so, list them out now, determine which will naturally diminish and which will need to be reduced.

Business Insurance Tips

Fire Insurance

- You can add other perils—such as windstorm, hail, smoke, explosion, vandalism, and malicious mischief—to your basic fire insurance at a relatively small additional fee.

- If you need comprehensive coverage, your best buy may be one of the all-risk contracts—such as the $1 million umbrella policy—that offers the broadest available protection for the money.

- Remember that the insurance company may compensate your losses by paying actual cash value of the property at the time of the loss, it may repair or replace the property with material of like kind and quality, or it may take all the property at the agreed or appraised value and reimburse you for your loss.

- Even if you have several policies on your property, you can still collect only the amount of your actual cash loss. All the insurers share the payment proportionately.

- Special protection other than the standard fire insurance policy is needed to cover the loss by fire of accounts, bills, currency, deeds, evidence of debt, and securities.

- After a loss, you must use all reasonable means to protect the property from further loss or run the risk of having your coverage canceled.

- In most cases, to recover your loss you must furnish within 60 days a complete inventory of the damaged, destroyed, and undamaged property showing in detail quantities, costs, actual cash value, and amount of loss claimed.

- If you and your insurer disagree on the amount of the loss, the question may be resolved through special appraisal procedures provided for in the fire insurance policy.

- You may cancel your policy without notice at any time and get part of the premium returned. The insurance company also may cancel at any time within a specified period, usually five days, with a written notice to you.

Liability Insurance

- You may be legally liable for damages even in cases where you used reasonable care.

- Under certain conditions, your business may be subject to damage claims even from trespassers.

- Most liability policies require you to notify the insurer immediately after an incident on your property that might cause a future claim. This holds true no matter how unimportant the incident may seem at the time it happens.

- Even if the suit against you is false or fraudulent, the liability insurer pays court costs, legal fees, and interest on judgments in addition to the liability judgments themselves.
- You can be liable for the acts of others under contracts you have signed with them, such as independent contractors. This liability is insurable.

Automobile Insurance

- When an employee uses a car on your behalf, you can be legally liable even though you don't own the car or truck.
- You can often get deductibles of almost any amount—$250, $500, $1,000—and thereby reduce your premiums.
- Automobile medical-payments insurance pays for medical claims, including your own, arising from vehicular accidents regardless of the question of negligence.
- In most states, you must carry liability insurance or be prepared to provide a surety bond or other proof of financial responsibility when you're involved in an accident.
- You can purchase uninsured motorist protection to cover your own bodily injury claims from someone who has no insurance.
- Personal property stored in a car or truck and not attached to it is not covered under an automobile policy.

Workers' Compensation Insurance

- Federal laws require that an employer provide employees a safe place to work, hire competent fellow employees, provide safe tools, and warn employees of existing danger. Whether or not an employer provides these things, he is liable for damage suits brought by an employee and possible fines or prosecution.
- State law determines the level or type of benefits payable under workers' compensation insurance policies.
- Not all employees are covered by workers' compensation insurance laws. The exceptions are determined by state law and therefore vary from state to state.
- You can save money on workers' compensation insurance by seeing that your employees are properly classified. Rates for workers' compensation insurance vary from 0.1 percent of the payroll for safe occupations to about 25 percent or more of the payroll for very hazardous occupations.
- Most employers can reduce their workers' compensation insurance premium cost by reducing their accident rates below the average. They do this by using safety and loss-prevention measures established by the individual state.

One successful travel service owner, while in a busy period, decided that times would be much slower six months hence. So he talked with his bank and other creditors, offering to pre-pay rent and computer expenses now so he could reduce payments later. It worked. When times got rougher, he reduced his expenses and weathered the problem.

If you aren't into your slow season yet, you can also talk to your lender about building a line of credit now that will help you get through the tougher times ahead.

Another source for cash to tide you through a recession is available from a second mortgage on your building, your home, or other large asset. Speak with your lender about this opportunity. Even if you decide not to take out a second mortgage, you will be ready if and when you need to do so.

Consider widening your market. That is, travel to a nearby metropolitan area and study whether you can expand your services to reach it. If so, you can pick up additional sales by either subcontracting your services or by promoting your services in the expanded market. It certainly beats starving at home.

Managing Expenses

Every dollar saved in overhead is a dollar on the bottom line of net profit—and a dollar less borrowed.

The object of reducing costs in your travel service business is to increase profits. Increasing profits through cost reduction must be based on the concept of an organized, planned program. Unless adequate records are maintained through an efficient and accurate accounting system, there can be no basis for analyzing costs.

Cost reduction is not simply attempting to slash any and all expenses without order. The owner-manager must understand the nature of expenses and how expenses interrelate with sales, inventories, overhead, gross profits, and net profits. Nor does cost reduction mean only the reduction of specific expenses. You can achieve greater profits through more efficient use of your expense dollar. Some of the ways you do this are by increasing the average sale per customer, by getting a larger return for your promotion and sales dollar, and by improving your internal methods and procedures.

As an example, one small travel agent was quite pleased when, in a single year, net sales went from $40,000 to $200,000. However, at the end of the year, records showed that net profit the prior year, with lower sales, was actually higher. Why? Because the expenses of doing business grew at a rate faster than the income.

Your goal should be to pay the right price for prosperity. Determining that price for your operation goes beyond knowing what your expenses are. Reducing expenses to increase profit requires that you obtain the most efficient use of your expense dollars.

Checking job records, you might determine that one of your employees is significantly less efficient than other employees performing the same tasks. You can then reduce expenses by increasing this employee's efficiency through training. By watching this employee perform his or her job, you can determine where the inefficiencies are and help him or her to overcome them. If done with consideration for the person, he or she will appreciate your attention, and so will your profit line.

Sometimes you cannot cut an expense item. But you can get more from it and thus increase your profits. In analyzing your expenses you should use percentages rather than actual dollar amounts. For example, if you increase sales and keep the dollar amount of an expense the same, you have decreased that expense as a percentage of income. When you decrease your cost percentage, you increase your percentage of profit.

On the other hand, if your sales volume remains the same, you can increase the percentage of profit by reducing a specific item of expense. Your goal, of course, is to simultaneously decrease specific expenses and increase their productive worth.

Before you can determine whether cutting expenses will increase profits, you need information about your operation. This information can be obtained only if you adequately use record-keeping and financial management systems discussed earlier.

Locating Reducible Expenses

Your income statement provides a summary of expense information and is the focal point in locating expenses that can be cut. For this reason, the information should be as current as possible. As a report of what has already been spent, an income statement alerts you to expense items that should be watched in the present business period. If you get an income statement only at the end of the year, you should consider having one prepared more often. At the end of each quarter is usually sufficient for smaller firms. Larger travel services should receive the information on a monthly basis.

Regardless of the frequency, the best option is to prepare two income statements. One statement should report the sales, expenses, profit, and loss of your operations cumulatively for the current business year to date. The other statement should report on the same items for the last complete month or quarter. Each of the statements should also carry the following information:

- This year's figures and each item as a percentage of sales
- Last year's figures and the percentages
- The difference between last year and this year—over or under
- Budgeted figures and the respective percentages
- The difference between current year actuals and the budgeted figures—over or under

- Average percentages for similar businesses (available from trade associations and the U.S. Department of Labor)
- The difference between your annual percentages and the industry ratios—over or under

This information allows you to locate expense variations in three ways:

1. By comparing this year to last year

2. By comparing expenses to your own budgeted figures

3. By comparing your percentages to the operating ratios for similar businesses

The important basis for comparison is the percentage figure. It represents a common denominator for all three methods. When you have indicated the percentage variations, you should then study the dollar amounts to determine what kind of corrective action is needed.

Because your cost cutting will come largely from variable expenses, you should make sure that they are indicated on your income statements. Variable expenses are those that fluctuate with the increase or decrease of sales volume. Some of them are overtime, temporary help, advertising, salaries, commissions, and payroll taxes. Fixed expenses are those that stay the same regardless of sales volume. Among them are your salary, salaries for permanent employees, depreciation, rent, and utilities.

When you have located a problem expense area, the next step obviously is to reduce that cost so as to increase your profit. A key to the effectiveness of your cost-cutting action is the worth of the various expenditures. As long as you know the worth of your expenditures, you can profit by making small improvements in expenses. Keep an open eye and an open mind. It is better to do a spot analysis once a month than to wait several months and then do a detailed study.

Take action as soon as possible. You can refine your cost-cutting action as you go along. Be persistent. Results typically come slower than you might like. Keep in mind that only persistent analysis of your records and constant action can help keep expenses from eating up profit.

Cutting Overhead Costs

Business overhead is simply the cost of keeping your doors open. If your travel service business is located in your home, overhead costs are probably small. But if you have a shop, an office, and office personnel, your overhead is greater. It's also large if you have high debt to banks, suppliers, and backers.

The suggestion made earlier in this book was to start out small and let your growing business force you into larger quarters. That is, depending on your travel service market, start with an office in a corner of your home. Then, as business grows, take on greater obligations for additional overhead. If you build the customer's perception of quality with your product, you won't have to maintain impressive offices. Few customers will decide not to do business with you because your office is in your home. This is especially true if they aren't aware that you are working from home.

You can also reduce overhead by carefully watching the costs of supplies. Printed stationery is an excellent way to promote the quality of your business, but you don't need printed notepads unless the customer will see them. For the price of generic ink pens you can often get ones that include your business name and phone number. But don't buy so many that they wind up costing more than quality ink pens because you've changed your address or phone number. Buy supplies in quantity if you can, but don't buy more than you will use in three to six months unless you're certain that they won't become out-of-date.

Travel expenses can easily get out of hand without good record keeping. That means developing a simple system for tracking transportation, lodging, meals, phone, and other costs.

Labor cost is one expense that can quickly eat away the profits of a small travel service business. Don't hire an office manager or secretary until you absolutely must. It's more profitable to do the required filing and office functions yourself after normal business hours or on weekends. Or you can ask the help of a spouse or older child who could be put on the payroll as soon as your business can afford it.

Some small travel services use temporary help or outside services rather than hire employees and deal with all the taxes and records that come with them. They have records kept by a bookkeeping or accounting service, office cleaning is done by a janitorial service (or the boss), telephones are answered by an answering service, correspondence and retyping service is performed by a secretarial service. Travel service jobs that the owner can't handle are contracted out to other travel agents or outside agents. They know that the complexity of regulations and taxation is endlessly multiplied when the first employee is hired—so they avoid hiring anyone until their success requires them to do so.

Long-distance phone calls can quickly add to your expenses and cut into your profits—especially when they are personal calls made by employees. Many successful travel services use a telephone call record to keep track of long-distance calls, then compare the report with the monthly phone bill. Calls not listed on the report are assumed to be personal calls and should be checked out.

One successful travel service makes sure all employees use toll-free numbers or calls travel suppliers collect whenever possible.

Managing the Future

As your travel service grows, there are many new elements to your task of managing a successful business. You must consider and plan for the loss of a key person or the business structure. You must remind yourself to enjoy what you're doing. You must review your options if the business fails. You must consider the long-term and begin planning for retirement. Planning well for tomorrow can reduce your worries today.

Succession in a Proprietorship

The personal skills, reputation, and management ability of the sole proprietor help to make the business successful. Without these human values the business is worth only the liquidation value of the tangible assets.

The sole proprietor's personal and business assets are one and the same. When a proprietor dies, the loss can become a financial disaster to the estate and the business. The business that was producing a good living for the owner and family will become a defunct business. What are the options?

The business may be transferred to a capable family member as a gift through provisions in the proprietor's will or by a sale provided through a prearranged purchase agreement effective at death. Cash is needed to offset losses to the business caused by the owner's death, to equalize the value of bequests made to other family members if the transfer is a gift, and to provide the sale price if the transfer is through sale.

If the buyer is a key employee, competitor, or third party, the business may be transferred at death, based on a prearranged sale agreement. However, cash is needed to provide a business continuation fund to meet expenses and perhaps to offset losses until the business adjusts to the new management.

If future management is not available then the business must be liquidated. Cash is needed to offset the difference between the business's going-concern value and its auction-block liquidation value, to provide a fund for income replacement to the family, and to pay outstanding business debts.

Succession in a Partnership

Unless there is a written agreement to the contrary, the death of a partner automatically dissolves the firm. In the absence of such an agreement, surviving partners have no right to buy the deceased's partnership interest. Surviving partners cannot assume the goodwill or take over the assets without consent of the deceased partner's estate. If the deceased was in debt to the partnership, the estate must settle the account in full and in cash.

The surviving partners act as liquidating trustees. They have exclusive possession of firm property but no right to carry on the business. If the business is continued, the surviving partners must share all profits with the deceased partner's estate and are liable for all losses. They must convert everything into cash at the best price obtainable. They must make an accounting to the deceased's estate and divide the proceeds with the estate. They must liquidate themselves out of their business and income.

What are the options a business has on the death of one of its partners?

If the surviving partner and deceased's heirs do nothing, the business is liquidated, resulting in auction price value for the salable assets. The business may receive nothing for goodwill. This is a disastrous solution for both the deceased partner's family and the surviving partners. It means termination of jobs for the surviving partners and employees.

The surviving partners may attempt to reorganize the partnership by taking the heirs into the partnership. But if heirs are unable to work in the business, the surviving partners must do all the work and share the profits. They could accept a new partner picked by the heirs. The surviving partners could also sell their interest in the business to the heirs, or conversely, buy out the heirs' interest.

Of course, there are some preparations that can be made prior to the death of a partner that will make a reorganization smoother. Buy and sell agreements funded with life insurance should be entered into while all partners are alive. Such an agreement, drafted by an attorney, will typically include a commitment by each partner not to dispose of his or her interest without first offering it at an agreed sale price to the partnership. The agreement will also include a provision for the partnership to buy a deceased partner's interest. The funding of the purchase will typically be from the proceeds of a life insurance policy written for that specific purpose.

Succession in a Corporation

The death of a stockholder who has been active in the operation of a closely held corporation allows the business entity to continue its legal structure, but not its personal structure. The interests of the heirs of the deceased inevitably come in conflict with the interests of the surviving associates.

What options are available to surviving stockholders?

The deceased's family may retain the stock interest. If the heirs have a majority interest, they may choose to become personally involved in management in order to receive income. Or they may choose to remain inactive, elect a new board of directors, and force the company to pay dividends. In either case, the surviving stockholders may lose a voice in management and possibly their jobs, while the deceased's family may become heirs to a business on the brink of failure. If the heirs have a minority interest and are not employed by the surviving associates, their only means of receiving an income from the corporation will be through dividends.

After the death of a stockholder, the deceased's heirs or estate may offer to sell the stock interest to the surviving stockholders. Or an outside buyer may be interested in purchasing stock in the corporation. While all of the interested parties are alive, they can enter into a binding buy and sell agreement funded with life insurance. This is done with a stockholder's buy and sell agreement drawn up with the assistance of your corporate attorney and accountant.

Succession in a Limited Liability Company

A limited liability company is similar in structure to a partner-ship. Therefore, partners should provide for the contingency of one another's death, incapacity, or desire to sell equity in the partnership agreement or in a buy and sell agreement. In the absence of such an agreement, surviving partners have no right nor obligation to buy the deceased's partnership interest. If the surviving partner and deceased's heirs do nothing, the business is liquidated, resulting in auction price value for the salable assets.

Buy and sell agreements should be entered into while all partners are alive. The agreement will include a commitment by each partner not to dispose of his or her interest without first offering it at an agreed sale price to the partnership. The agreement will also include a provision for the partnership to buy a deceased partner's interest. The purchase is usually funded from the proceeds of a life insurance policy written for that specific purpose.

Death of Key Employees

Many growing firms develop key employees who represent assets the firm cannot afford to be without. Even though these key employees may not own an interest in the firm, they are nonetheless valuable to its continuation. So what happens if a key employee dies?

Travel services with key employees should consider life insurance payable to the firm on the death or disability of these people. How much life insurance? It should be an amount sufficient to offset financial losses during the readjustment period, to retain good credit standing, and to assure customers and suppliers that the company will continue as usual. In addition, key-employee insurance could retire loans, mortgages, bonds, attract and train a successor, or carry out ongoing plans for expansion and new developments. Talk to your insurance agent about the appropriate policy for insuring your business against the loss of a proprietor, a partner, a stockholder, or a key employee. It's one of the costs of growth.

Traveling for Business and Pleasure

George Moore once suggested, "A man travels the world over in search of what he needs, and returns home to find it."

The primary reason you started (or will start) your own travel business was to increase your opportunities to enjoy life. You wanted to offer a needed service, you wanted to help others, you wanted to extend your business skills, and you wanted to be able to afford to travel. However, you didn't want to spend your entire waking time working. In fact, you may get so caught up in the chase for success that you miss the opportunities that success brings along the way.

Those who have found success in the travel service and other fields will tell you that success is often empty if not shared with others. And that doesn't mean waiting until a successful destination—say at $1 million net worth—is reached. It means sharing success with others along the way, on a day-to-day basis. Maybe, for you, this means sharing your success with your family, a few good friends, or a charitable organization. In any case, consider that your financial success will mean much more to you if you can use it to bring physical, emotional, or spiritual success to others.

Manage your life outside your business as you do your time at the business. Look for ways of helping others. Find methods of giving yourself the things you most enjoy, whether time with friends, time with hobbies, time with competitive sports, time alone, or all of the above. Take advantage of familiarization or fam trips and discount passes offered by airlines, resorts, and others. Especially, take time to recharge your batteries. You will use lots of personal energy in starting, managing, and growing your travel service business. Make sure you take the time to reenergize yourself.

When to Quit

The failure rate of new businesses is very high. It lowers as your travel service matures. The longer you're in business, the greater the chance that you will continue in business. However, your travel service business can fail at any time, quite often due to poor record keeping. So a key element of continued success is maintaining good records and learning how to manage by them.

But there may come a time when business conditions require that you throw in the towel. If you're not making sufficient profit or are reducing your capital to losses, you will soon be in financial trouble. What to do?

First, cut overhead as much as possible. The sooner this is done, the longer your business will survive—maybe long enough to find a solution.

Next, sell unused or inefficient assets. Of course, you must maintain your working tools. But maybe you can move your office to a less expensive location—even back home.

Then talk with your creditors about the situation and what you plan to do. Some may be very helpful in offering a workable solution—an extension of credit, assistance in finding additional contracts, or even purchase of stock in your business.

Finally, as necessary, talk with your attorney about your legal obligations and options. No one wants to declare bankruptcy, but it may be necessary. Or you may decide to set up a payment schedule for all debts and return to the work force as an employee.

There is no shame in failing to succeed—just in failing to try. If there are things you've learned from the experience, you can use them to increase your worth to an employer. Who better to manage a travel service business than one who has learned what doesn't work.

Of course, now that you've planned out how to minimize losses, you probably won't have to. In fact, you can look forward to retirement.

Planning to Retire

When should you retire from your profitable travel service business? When you want to. Some travel agents will hold off retiring until they are no longer physically able to work their trade. Others make plans to retire when they are 65 or even 62 years of age. Still others give their business 10 or 20 years to grow, then sell it to semiretire or move to a different trade. Some work their children into it, then gradually turn it over to them.

Some successful travel service business owners will sell their shares to a partner or to another agency. Others will sell or give their equity in the business to a relative. Some will sell out to key employees or to competitors.

The business can be sold outright for cash, earning the owner a cash settlement for his equity; or the seller can carry the paper or sell it on a contract with a downpayment and monthly payments for a specified term. In this case, buyers will often require the seller to sign a noncompetition contract that says the seller can't go to work for a competing travel service or start another travel service business in the same market.

Action Guidelines

This is the end of the beginning. You now have many of the tools you need to start and succeed with your own travel service. Here's how you can put this final chapter into action:

✔ Apply the problem-solving techniques in this chapter to a current problem that your travel service is facing or expects to face.

✔ Even if you don't plan to hire anyone, review the methods of managing employees. If nothing else, it will remind you of why you don't want to increase your staff for awhile.

✔ If you have or expect to hire employees, review the information on benefits programs to determine which best fit your business and philosophy.

✔ Find a local temporary employment office who may be able to help you during busy times.

✔ Find qualified outside travel agents whom you can contract with as your business gets busier.

✔ Consult with your insurance agent to make sure you are not undercovered or overbilled.

✔ Plan today for how your business will survive the death of a principal, partner, or key employee.

✔ Periodically review your expenses to ensure you are getting the most from each dollar you spend.

✔ Have fun with your travel service and your life!

RESOURCES
FOR SMALL BUSINESS

These publications on proven management techniques for small businesses are available from Upstart Publishing Company, Inc., 155 North Wacker Drive, Chicago, IL 60606. For a free current catalog of small business books and resources, call (800) 829-7934 or (312) 836-4400, ext. 650 in Illinois.

The Business Planning Guide, 6th edition, 1992, David H. Bangs, Jr. and Upstart Publishing Company, Inc. A manual that helps you write a business plan and financing proposal tailored to your business, your goals, and your resources. Includes worksheets and checklists. (Softcover, 208 pp., $19.95)

The Market Planning Guide, 4th edition, 1994, David H. Bangs, Jr. and Upstart Publishing Company, Inc. A manual to help small-business owners put together a goal-oriented, resource-based marketing plan with action steps, benchmarks and time lines. Includes worksheets and checklists to make implementation and review easier. (Softcover, 180 pp., $19.95)

The Cash Flow Control Guide, 1990, David H. Bangs, Jr. and Upstart Publishing Company, Inc. A manual to help small-business owners solve their number one financial problem. Includes worksheets and checklists. (Softcover, 88 pp., $14.95)

The Personnel Planning Guide, 1988, David H. Bangs, Jr. and Upstart Publishing Company, Inc. A 176-page manual outlining practical, proven personnel management techniques, including hiring, managing, evaluating and compensating personnel. Includes worksheets and checklists. (Softcover, 176 pp., $19.95)

The Start Up Guide: A One-Year Plan for Entrepreneurs, 2nd edition, 1994, David H. Bangs, Jr. and Upstart Publishing Company, Inc. This book utilizes the same step-by-step, no-jargon method as *The Business Planning Guide,* to help even those with no business training through the process of beginning a successful business. (Softcover, 176 pp., $19.95)

Managing By the Numbers: Financial Essentials for the Growing Business, 1992, David H. Bangs, Jr. and Upstart Publishing Company, Inc. Straightforward techniques for getting the maximum return with a minimum of detail in your business's financial management. (Softcover, 160 pp., $19.95)

Building Wealth, 1992, David H. Bangs, Jr. and the editors of *Common Sense.* A collection of tested techniques designed to help you plan your personal finances and how to plan your business finances to benefit you, your family, and employees. (Softcover, 168 pp., $19.95)

Buy the Right Business—At the Right Price, 1990, Brian Knight and the Associates of Country Business, Inc. Many people who would like to be in business for themselves think strictly of starting a business. In some cases, buying a going concern may be preferable—and just as affordable. (Softcover, 152 pp., $18.95)

Borrowing for Your Business, 1991, George M. Dawson. This is a book for borrowers and about lenders. Includes detailed guidelines on how to select a bank and a banker, how to answer the lender's seven most important questions, how your banker looks at a loan, and how to get a loan renewed. (Hardcover, 160 pp., $19.95)

Can This Partnership Be Saved? 1992, Peter Wylie and Mardy Grothe. The authors offer solutions and hope for problems between key people in business. (Softcover, 272 pp., $19.95)

Cases in Small Business Management, 1994, John Edward de Young. A compilation of intriguing and useful case studies in typical small business problems. (Softcover, 258 pp., $24.95)

The Complete Guide to Selling Your Business, 1992, Paul Sperry and Beatrice Mitchell. A step-by-step guide through the entire process from how to determine when the time is right to sell to negotiating the final terms. (Hardcover, 160 pp., $21.95)

The Complete Selling System, 1991, Pete Frye. This book can help any manager or salesperson, even those with no experience, find the solutions to some of the most common dilemmas in managing sales. (Hardcover, 192 pp., $21.95)

Creating Customers, 1992, David H. Bangs, Jr. and the editors of *Common Sense.* A book for business owners and managers who want a step-by-step approach to selling and promoting. Techniques include inexpensive market research, pricing your goods and services and writing a usable marketing plan. (Softcover, 176 pp., $19.95)

The Entrepreneur's Guide to Going Public, 1994, James B. Arkebauer with Ron Schultz. A comprehensive and useful book on a subject that is the ultimate dream of most entrepreneurs—making an initial public offering (IPO). (Softcover, 368 pp., $19.95)

Export Profits, 1992, Jack S. Wolf. This book shows how to find the right foreign markets for your product, cut through the red tape, minimize currency risks, and find the experts who can help. (Softcover, 304 pp., $19.95)

Financial Troubleshooting, 1992, David H. Bangs, Jr. and the editors of *Common Sense.* This book helps the owner/manager use basic diagnostic methods to monitor the health of the business and solve problems before damage occurs. (Softcover, 192 pp., $19.95)

Financial Essentials for Small Business Success, 1994, Joseph Tabet and Jeffrey Slater. Designed to show readers where to get the information they need and how planning and recordkeeping will enhance the health of any small business. (Softcover, 272 pp., $19.95)

From Kitchen to Market, 1992, Stephen Hall. A practical approach to turning culinary skills into a profitable business. (Softcover, 208 pp., $24.95)

The Home-Based Entrepreneur, 1993, Linda Pinson and Jerry Jinnett. A step-by-step guide to all the issues surrounding starting a home-based business. Issues such as zoning, labor laws, and licensing are discussed and forms are provided to get you on your way. (Softcover, 192 pp., $19.95)

Keeping the Books, 1993, Linda Pinson and Jerry Jinnett. Basic business recordkeeping both explained and illustrated. Designed to give you a clear understanding of small business accounting by taking you step-by-step through general records, development of financial statements, tax reporting, scheduling, and financial statement analysis. (Softcover, 208 pp., $19.95)

The Language of Small Business, 1994, Carl O. Trautmann. A clear, concise dictionary of small business terms for students and small business owners. (Softcover, 416 pp., $19.95)

Marketing Your Invention, 1992, Thomas Mosley. This book dispels the myths and clearly communicates what inventors need to know to successfully bring their inventions to market. (Softcover, 232 pp., $19.95)

100 Best Retirement Businesses, 1994, Lisa Angowski Rogak with David H. Bangs, Jr. A one-of-a-kind book bringing retirees the inside information on the most interesting and most lucrative businesses for them. (Softcover, 416 pp., $15.95)

The Small Business Computer Book, 1993, Robert Moskowitz. This book does not recommend particular systems, but rather provides readers with a way to think about these choices and make the right decisions for their businesses. (Softcover, 190 pp., $19.95)

Start Your Own Business for $1,000 or Less, 1994, Will Davis. Shows readers how to get started in the "mini-business" of their dreams with less than $1,000. (Softcover, 280 pp., $17.95)

Steps to Small Business Start-Up, 1993, Linda Pinson and Jerry Jinnett. A step-by-step guide for starting and succeeding with a small or home-based business. Takes you through the mechanics of business startup and gives an overview of information on such topics as copyrights, trademarks, legal structures, recordkeeping, and marketing. (Softcover, 256 pp., $19.95)

Target Marketing for the Small Business, 1993, Linda Pinson and Jerry Jinnett. A comprehensive guide to marketing your business. This book not only shows you how to reach your customers, it also gives you a wealth of information on how to research that market through the use of library resources, questionnaires, demographics, etc. (Softcover, 176 pp., $19.95)

On Your Own: A Woman's Guide to Starting Your Own Business, 2nd edition, 1993, Laurie Zuckerman. *On Your Own is* for women who want hands-on, practical information about starting and running their own business. It deals honestly with issues like finding time for your business when you're also the primary care provider, societal biases against women and credit discrimination. (Softcover, 320 pp., $19.95)

Problem Employees, 1991, Dr. Peter Wylie and Dr. Mardy Grothe. Provides managers and supervisors with a simple, practical and straightforward approach to help all employees, especially problem employees, significantly improve their work performance. (Softcover, 272 pp., $22.95)

Problems and Solutions in Small Business Management, 1994, the editors of *Forum,* the journal of the Association of Small Business Development Centers. A collection of case studies selected from the pages of *Forum* magazine. (Softcover, 200 pp., $21.95)

The Restaurant Planning Guide, 1992, Peter Rainsford and David H. Bangs, Jr. This book takes the practical techniques of *The Business Planning Guide* and combines it with the expertise of Peter Rainsford, a restaurateur and a professor at the Cornell School of Hotel Administration. Topics include: establishing menu prices, staffing and scheduling, controlling costs and niche marketing. (Softcover, 176 pp., $19.95)

Successful Retailing, 2nd edition, 1993, Paula Wardell. Provides hands-on help for those who want to start or expand their retail business. Sections include: strategic planning, marketing and market research and inventory control. (Softcover, 176 pp., $19.95)

The Upstart Guide to Owning and Managing an Antiques Business, 1994, Lisa Angowski Rogak. Provides the information a prospective antiques dealer needs to run a business profitably. (Softcover, 224 pp., $15.95)

The Upstart Guide to Owning and Managing a Bar or Tavern, 1994, Roy Alonzo. Provides essential information on planning, making the initial investment, financial management, and marketing a bar or tavern. (Softcover, 256 pp., $15.95)

The Upstart Guide to Owning and Managing a Bed & Breakfast, 1995, Lisa Angowski Rogak. Provides information on choosing the best location, licensing and what really goes on behind the scenes. (Softcover, 224 pp., $15.95)

The Upstart Guide to Owning and Managing a Consulting Service, 1995, Dan Ramsey. Gives the reader all he or she needs to become a successful consultant to businesses or consumers, with resource lists, how to find prospects, and financial and tax advice. (Softcover, 224 pp., $ 15.95)

The Upstart Guide to Owning and Managing a Desktop Publishing Service, 1995, Dan Ramsey. Explains how anyone with a flair for words, a sense of graphic design, and a willingness to buy a good computer can start a desktop publishing business. (Softcover, 201 pp., $15.95)

The Upstart Guide to Owning and Managing a Florist Service, 1995, Dan Ramsey. Provides information on starting up a full-service florist business, including information on location, setup of the actual flower shop, and lists of resources and suppliers. (Softcover, 224 pp., $ 15.95)

The Upstart Guide to Owning and Managing a Résumé Service, 1995, Dan Ramsey. Shows how any reader can turn personnel, writing, and computer skills into a lucrative résumé-writing business. (Softcover, 224 pp., $15.95)

The Upstart Guide to Owning and Managing a Newsletter Business, 1995, Lisa Angowski Rogak. All the reader needs to begin a newsletter business, including topics, how to do a market analysis, what equipment to buy, and daily operations information. Extensive resources and a business plan, too. (Softcover, 224 pp., $15.95)

The Woman Entrepreneur, 1992, Linda Pinson and Jerry Jinnett. Thirty-three successful women business owners share their practical ideas for success and their sources for inspiration. (Softcover, 244 pp., $14.00)

Other Available Titles

The Complete Guide to Business Agreements, 1993, Ted Nicholas, Enterprise • Dearborn. Contains 127 of the most commonly needed business agreements. (Loose-leaf binder, $69.95)

The Complete Small Business Legal Guide, 1993, Robert Friedman, Enterprise • Dearborn. Provides the hands-on help you need to start a business, maintain all necessary records, properly hire and fire employees, and deal with the many changes a business goes through. (Loose-leaf binder, $69.95)

Guerrilla Marketing: Secrets for Making Big Profits from Your Small Business, 1984, J. Conrad Levinson, Houghton-Mifflin. A classic tool kit for small businesses. (Hardcover, 226 pp., $14.95)

How to Form Your Own Corporation Without a Lawyer for Under $75.00, 1992, Ted Nicholas, Enterprise • Dearborn. A good book for helping you to discover all the unique advantages of incorporating while at the same time learning how quick, easy, and inexpensive the process can be. (Softcover, $19.95)

Marketing Sourcebook for Small Business, 1989, Jeffrey P. Davidson, John Wylie Publishing. A good introductory book for small business owners with excellent definitions of important marketing terms and concepts. (Hardcover, 325 pp., $24.95)

***The Small Business Survival Kit: 101 Troubleshooting Tips
for Success,*** 1993, John Ventura, Enterprise • Dearborn.
Offers compassionate insight into the emotional side of financial difficulties as well as a nuts-and-bolts consideration of
options for the small businessperson experiencing tough times.
(Softcover, $19.95)

INDEX

Hotels, 12
Humor, stress relief and, 21

I
IBM AT, 24
IBM OS/2, 27
IBM XT, 24
ICTA (Institute of Certified Travel Agents), 48
IFA (International Franchise Association), 52
Immigration Reform and Control Act of 1986, 68-69
Impressions, advertising and, 121
Income, 12-13
Income Opportunities, 52
Income statement, 81, 133, 134-135, 150, 151
Incorporation, 76-78
Independence, 20
Independent contractors, 169-170
Independent tours, 6
Indirect expenses, 134-135
Information Age, 7
Insolvency, 139
Institute of Certified Travel Agents (ICTA), 48
Insurance. *See also specific types of insurance,* partnership, 75; against risks, 172-175
Insurance agent, hiring of, 82-83
Integrated software programs, 29-30
Intel Pentium microprocessor, 24
Interest costs, 137
Interest rates, managing, 146-148
Internal Revenue Service (IRS), 39; forms, 109-110; payroll systems and, 101; publications, 55, 109, 166
Schedule SE, 109
International Airlines Travel Agent Network, 48
International Air Traffic Association, 38
International Franchise Association (IFA), 52

International Tours, 51
Investments, 142
IRS. *See* Internal Revenue Service (IRS)

J
Job applicants, sources of, 106-107
Job application, 69-71
Job description, 106
Judgment, 21

L
Labor costs, 12-13, 181
Labor expenses, 13-14
Landlord, 67
Laser printers, 31
Lease, 67
Leisure Resource, 50
Lenders, 74
Leverage, 151
Leverage ratio, 153
Liabilities, 98, 135, 136, 137
Liability accounts, 98
Liability insurance, 83, 173, 174-175
Life insurance, 184, 185-186
Life insurance loan, 146
Limited liability company (LLC), 78-79, 185
Line of credit, 139, 144
Liquidation of business, 182-183
Liquidity, 151
Liquidity ratios, 151
Litigation, 83
LLC (limited liability company), 78-79, 185
Loan officer, questions of, 143-144
Loans, 81-82, 143-146. *See also specific types of loans;* applications for, 149-150; interest rates and, 146-148; line of credit, 144; SBA guaranteed, 148-150; signature, 144
Local merchants association, 67
Location, factors in selecting, 63-66; retail compatibility and, 66-67; selection of, 66-67; in shopping mall, 66; zoning laws and, 67-68